In *Story Thinking,* John once again pulls together some deep thinking into a very powerful model and concept that provides a keen and workable insight for KMers and for anyone focused on human achievement in the Knowledge Age, where "learning is not an 'add-on' to business, but the way of business."
— **Douglas Weidner, Executive Chairman, Chief CKM Instructor, International Knowledge Management Institute, LLC**

The *Story Thinking* model is an evidence-based model for change that allows the reader to focus their thinking more towards *change* as a constant. This is something we all need to be practicing in almost every facet of work and life.
— **Rose Noxon, PhD, CPT, President, International Society for Performance Improvement**

John Lewis has written an important new book on *story thinking* and sensemaking, including sections on change, learning, and leadership. The purpose of John's book is to prepare organizations for a fourth industrial revolution based on a new capacity to change and learn. *Story Thinking* can be applied by knowledge managers, change agents, learning professionals, and leaders of all kinds.
— **Stan Garfield, Knowledge Management author, speaker, and community leader**

Once again, John Lewis has shortcut the path to more effective leadership – and more effective organizations.
— **Joe Mason, Chief Marketing Officer, Allianz Partners**

There is no shortage of books on leadership, including books on using storytelling to paint a clear vision of the future. But getting there also requires innovation, learning, team formation, change management, and execution. Books for each of these topics by themselves are in plentiful supply. But nobody has managed to stitch them all together into a single, coherent narrative, until now. Backed by solid research and practical experience, this is a *must read* for leaders seeking to thrive in the whirlwind of change.
— **Dr. Art Murray, CEO, Applied Knowledge Sciences, Inc. and author,** *"Building the Enterprise of the Future: Co-creating and delivering extraordinary value in an eight-billion-mind world"*

I love how John's book is centered on problem-solving and how this leads to learning with stories. When creating a collaboration program, these elements are the best way to start, sustain, and create a world class collaboration ecosystem.

— Dan Ranta, Knowledge Management Leader at GE

Story Thinking reveals prescient insight into the future of work and presents an agile approach to describing and managing change. The *story thinking* cycle focuses on making change compelling and attractive; the process encourages a forward-leaning emotional connection with opportunities and solutions that will yield a better future. John Lewis' models explain how using the sensemaking pattern of stories to explore options and their consequences can transform the results organizations achieve.

— Ralph Poole, Engagement Director and Senior Consultant at Iknow LLC., and Knowledge Management Professor

Whether you are in a new career or wanting to take your career to the next level, this book is for you. John's *Story Thinking* paradigm for problem solving, innovation, and leadership provides immediately useful guidance for today as well as the coming fourth industrial revolution. I know this groundbreaking approach works because I apply these principles in my personal and professional life daily.

— Eric F. Palmer, Director of Web Services, University of Richmond

The inimitable John Lewis has struck home again, helping us move beyond storytelling to *story thinking*, enabling us to better link patterns from the past to the continuing exploration of an emerging future. Lewis takes *story thinking* into the realms of change, learning and leadership, providing real application examples and challenging us to break old paradigms and engage new ways of thinking and acting. While this trip is recursive throughout life, as Lewis states, "Some trips around this cycle take only a moment, some require a project, and some can take a lifetime." And whether you choose to take the short track or long trek, you will discover the usefulness of Lewis' Learning Objective Framework and Key Performance Indicators to help ensure the success of your journey. This is a book worth reading.

— Alex Bennet, PhD, Founder, Mountain Quest Institute, and Professor of Knowledge and Innovation Management, Bangkok University

Story Thinking

Transforming Organizations for the
Fourth Industrial Revolution

John Lewis

Author of *The Explanation Age*

Independently Published via Amazon KDP.

ISBN: 9781088545850

Printed in the United States of America.

For the thinkers, truth-seekers, and thought leaders

"Within the second industrial revolution, we became accustomed to saying that everything happens within a process—and the framework of "process" became our mental model of work.

Now, in the fourth industrial revolution, we will need to understand that the framework of "story" must become our mental model of work.

Storytelling is based on a sensemaking pattern for how we should talk—but Story Thinking is based on this sensemaking pattern for how we should work."

Contents

Introduction

This book is about the major organizational challenges related to the Fourth Industrial Revolution (4IR), and ways for visionary leaders to begin addressing them now by rethinking traditional views of change, learning, and leadership. This is not another book about the gloom and doom associated with predicted job losses due to robots and artificial intelligence (AI). Instead, this is a solutions-based book that provides a new way of thinking about the organization, called *Story Thinking*.

The first industrial revolution was based on *steam* and mechanical production. The second revolution was based on *electricity* and assembly lines. The third revolution was based on *computing* and online workflow. All three of these technological advancements completely changed the underlying approaches towards business. But the next revolution will be even more profound. The fourth revolution is primarily based on *intelligence* and digital connectivity. This will move us beyond building a workforce *around* the technology—the workforce will also be *competing* with the technology. Successful organizations will need to do more than just adopt smarter tools—they will need to adopt smarter ways of thinking beyond current memorized prescriptive change models.

Within the *second* industrial revolution, we became accustomed to saying that everything happens within a process—and the framework of "process" became our mental model of work. Now, in the *fourth* industrial revolution, we will need to understand that the framework of "story" must become our mental model of work. *Storytelling* is based on a sensemaking pattern for how we should talk—but *Story Thinking* is based on this sensemaking pattern for how we should *work*.

As a consultant and professor of change, learning, and knowledge management, the Fourth Industrial Revolution presents an exciting challenge. While others are writing on the expected negative impacts to the workforce, I wanted to write a book about the opportunity we have for organizations and individuals. Years ago, before most people had heard of GPS (Global Positioning System), I had the opportunity to work on the team that launches and operates the GPS satellites. Instead of looking through maps and memorizing navigational directions, this technology connects our knowledge of the landscape with our goals and required actions. When working on my doctoral dissertation, I wanted to apply the same approach to how organizations operate and learn. The power of knowing "You Are Here" can be extended beyond geography, to provide a shared mental model for the core functions of an organization.

As Klaus Schwab, Executive Chairman of the World Economic Forum, created a picture of how emerging technologies will come together, he presented us with some interesting organizational challenges in his book, *The Fourth Industrial Revolution* (Schwab, 2017). He says companies will need to "rethink their operating models" and overcome their "lack of understanding of the nature of disruptive changes." In fact, the "first imperative of the business impact" is to assess the current capacity to *change* and *learn*. And as distributed teams represent distributed decision-making, he says that "governments are among the most impacted" and will need to "engage citizens more effectively" and "conduct policy experiments that allow for learning and adaptation."

To address these challenges, my book is organized into three parts. The *first* part is about *Change*, which is really the constant within our organizations. Here, we compare transformational and transactional change, visualize the underlying mindsets that produce change, and rethink the tasks of strategic planning and continuous improvement using the ILEDEM ("I led 'em") model. The *second* part is about *Learning*, which goes way beyond training. Here, we visualize continuous feedback with the "Quad-Loop" Learning framework, replace Bloom's Taxonomy for formal education, and see how to develop Thought Leaders instead of just Experts using the "Learning S-Curve." The *third* part is about *Leadership*, which is based on a "Learner Leader" model. Here, we connect knowledge management systems with learning organizations, visualize decision transparency with the "Option Outline," and understand the sensemaking process of transparent policy-making. I conclude each chapter with specific questions, tasks, and tools, and summarize the book with the key principles for applying story thinking.

The purpose of this book is to prepare organizations for the Fourth Industrial Revolution with an optimistic view based on a new capacity to *change* and *learn.* I agree with the Forbes Magazine contributing author, Bernard Marr who says "Rather than succumb to the doomsday predictions that 'robots will take over all the jobs,' a more optimistic outlook is one where humans get the opportunity to do work that demands their creativity, imagination, social and emotional intelligence, and passion" (Marr, 2019). But the key to this outlook is having the right organizational operating model, the right definition of learning, and the right style of leadership. This is what you will find within Story Thinking.

I

PART I: CHANGE

1

Story-based Change

"We will never transform the prevailing system of management without transforming our prevailing system of education. They are the same system." — W. Edwards Deming

Q: Is the sensemaking pattern of stories just for how we should talk, or also for how we should work?

From Problem to Solution

How do people and organizations solve problems? How do they change, learn, and improve? If we picture an arrow connecting a problem to a solution (see figure 1.1), we really want to know what is inside that arrow. We expect a lot from this little arrow. If we knew what was inside it, we would know how we get from problems to solutions. We would have the magic formula for continuous improvement, innovation, and growth. So, what is inside the arrow?

Figure 1.1—The Arrow Between Problem and Solution

In getting "from problem to solution," the easiest, and the easiest to find, approach is to look for explanations that fill in the simple framework called "If/Then." Memorizing a rule allows us to simply identify the current problem ("IF this occurs") and match it with its solution ("THEN do this"). In his book, *Blink*, Malcolm Gladwell offers numerous examples where "decisions made very quickly can be every bit as good as decisions made cautiously and deliberately." But it is also possible, especially for non-experts, where these moments of "blink" can become moments of "blunder."

To expand beyond simple rules, some have tried to answer this question by creating "change models" which provide organizations with some steps to follow. The assumption is that if you simply follow the steps in the model then you will always get from your problem to your solution. So naturally, as each new change model is created, we send people from our organization to learn how to use the new magic formula. The idea is to become trained and certified as an official "step-follower" in the latest model. The typical *change* model from the first and second industrial revolutions is *prescriptive* in nature, meaning they provide some memorized steps to perform and sound like this: Do-These-Things-In-This-Order. This is like getting some navigational directions to memorize without a map to understand the overall layout of the landscape, how to reroute when the directions stop working, or where the directional steps originated from. The change models with memorized steps have provided us with some blind guidance for what is inside the arrow—but with little understanding.

While we have been busy trying to identify and follow the steps inside the arrow, we have also been busy trying to understand and communicate our journey. In his 1989 book, *Information Anxiety*, Richard Saul Wurman got it right in his description of the situation. Some think that information anxiety is simply due to the sheer *amount* of information that is available, but Wurman points to the real source of anxiety: the *gap* between "what we understand and what we *think* we should understand." And the gap has only grown since 1989. But luckily, we have found that when we use storytelling to describe our journey through the arrow, something magical happens. By communicating with stories, we find a sensemaking pattern that provides needed understanding which also resonates with others. Just as the brain can detect visual patterns, it can also detect the fundamental pattern in information—we are wired for stories (Fletcher, 1995). Now, as we try to follow the old Industrial Age change models in our organizations, at least we have the "story" to help us communicate our journey and frustrations for what appears to work and what seems to not work.

This brings us to an obvious question: What if the pattern of stories is not just for how we should *talk*? What if it is also for how we should *work*? What if the model we seek inside the arrow is the same sensemaking pattern found within the structure of stories? This is beyond storytelling—this is story thinking.

The Story Pattern

When watching a movie or listening to someone tell their story, there is a general pattern for how the story starts, how it evolves, and how it ends. This basic pattern, with a *beginning*, *middle*, and *ending*, has been known since Aristotle pointed it out to us about two thousand years ago in his book, *Poetics*. At the beginning of the story, there is a normalcy that becomes disrupted. This is followed by a discovery of the real issue and a plan for how to deal with it. Then the plan is hit with obstacles which are eventually overcome, providing a resolution, but also some transformation in the main character. The ending provides closure and a sense that "they live happily ever after," at least until the sequel arrives—but having withstood the change of the journey, somehow, and maybe necessarily, the main character has changed as well.

Story Thinking takes Aristotle's three-part description of our natural story-telling pattern and breaks it out into six phases of the cycle: Automation, Disruption, Investigation, Ideation, Expectation, and Affirmation—also called ADIIEA (pronounced uh-dee-uh). Starting from our normal routine (Automation), we encounter something out of the ordinary (Disruption) and begin to look deeper into the situation (Investigation). Then we think of some ideas (Ideation) and put a plan into action (Expectation). With a sound plan, we eventually see positive results (Affirmation), and over time, we settle into a new routine (Automation). Some trips around this cycle take only a moment, some require a project, and some can take a lifetime (Lewis, 2013).

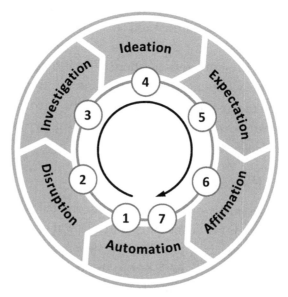

Figure 1.2—The Story Pattern

Here is an example of how someone would describe their story (see figure 1.2):

1. Automation: "I was doing my normal routine."
2. Disruption: "Then something out of the ordinary occurred."
3. Investigation: "I needed time to figure out what had really happened."
4. Ideation: "And then I got an idea."
5. Expectation: "I worked on my plan."
6. Affirmation: "And finally, success!"
7. Automation: "Now, I have a new and better routine."

The interesting thing is that when people show up to work, they expect work to make sense. They are not satisfied with rationale that simply says: "just follow the steps." When given a chance to tell a story about their business project, we can find the story thinking pattern within their work:

1. Automation: "We had successful operations at work."
2. Disruption: "But we knew more competition was coming."
3. Investigation: "We discovered a new idea that we could incorporate."
4. Ideation: "And created a new vision."
5. Expectation: "Development took some time."
6. Affirmation: "But it all came together!"
7. Automation: "Now operations are even better."

Klaus Schwab says in his book, *The Fourth Industrial Revolution*, "There has never been a time of greater promise or potential peril. My concern, however, is that decision-makers are too often caught in traditional, linear (and non-disruptive) thinking or too absorbed by immediate concerns to think strategically about the forces of disruption and innovation shaping our future." Story Thinking, as a visualization tool, provides insights into an underlying pattern to change, regardless if found in a personal story, or an account of a business project, which requires addressing Disruption as well as Ideation. It moves the story *about* change—to be *inside* the arrow of change. The appendix of this book provides a comparative view into 30 popular change models for how they align to the "unified model" of story thinking with six phases of change. Let's look at each of these six phases in more detail:

Automation is a *routine* state of mind, for individuals, organizations, and mechanized systems. As a state of mind, Automation is not just for AI (Artificial Intelligence) and robots; it also represents the mindless work that humans perform each day. This is the phase where we are operating on autopilot and status quo, to maximize our proficiency. This is also the phase that marks the *beginning* and the *end* of the transformational story cycle. As it rests at the bottom of the cycle, we are reminded that we tend to "settle" here, operating in a mentally mechanized state, hopefully in line with our goals for operational activities as well as maintenance activities, otherwise we will ensure we will end up in Disruption.

Disruption is the phase where we prepare for and respond to situations that are out of the ordinary. Disruption is fundamentally a reactionary state of mind, but we can prepare for risks and train with drills for how we will react if risks become real. A disruption can be a *problem*, or it can be recognized as an *opportunity*, which is how many innovations begin. A disruption can *happen* out of the blue—or can be *initiated* when the current status quo is no longer good enough. Given that we may have more than one disruption occurring at the same time, proper prioritization is also key for this phase.

Investigation is the phase where we are asking questions, as individuals and as an organization, about a situation that does not fit into the current status quo. Simply asking "What went wrong?" assumes there is only a *problem* and not an *opportunity*. The quality and depth of the questions asked in this phase are the key to effective analysis as well as discovery. Our ability to explore here is just as important as our ability to inspect and find root causes. Since the questions we ask will determine what we find, the key here is in keeping an open mind and an impartial approach.

Ideation is the phase where we are asking questions related to what "could work." Asking "what if" questions promotes innovative solutions, more than simply asking what your competition is doing. This is not just about "creativity" alone; Ideation may start with creative brainstorming and diversity of initial ideas, but it needs to conclude with a design and a plan that are realistic with thoughtful tradeoff decisions, which provide a clear picture and motivation to move into the Expectation phase.

Expectation is the phase where we are progressing against the plan and accomplishing deliverables. We understand, and can reflectively state, the ideas we hope for, and are going to put our faith in, because we believe they "could work." Expectation requires a reflective state of mind, where we are deliberately acting with intention and purpose, as compared to our mindless actions in Automation. With enough persistence here, we eventually reach Affirmation.

Affirmation is the phase where we satisfy doubt by reflectively testing and knowing that something is "true" or "does work." If something still needs more work, we just need to go back to Expectation until we are ready to test it again. We eventually begin trusting these answers as "fact" so we can simply reference or memorize them, instead of constantly testing and "reinventing the wheel." Eventually, the ideas that we trust do not need to be looked up or referenced—they become codified into our routine and the cycle ends where it begins, in Automation.

In researching the nature of *sensemaking*, some have taken a "micro" approach by studying *detailed* decision steps like watching how people solve puzzles. But, instead of taking this laboratory approach, Gary Klein et al. (2003) study the topic of "macrocognition" which involves higher-level "cognitive functions that are performed in *natural* decision-making settings." They propose that *storybuilding* is a "supporting strategy" during naturalistic decision making, and that these higher-level tasks include problem detection, constructing options, and working in uncertainty. This is the level that this book addresses within the arrow between "problem and solution." Without an underlying map, we are lost, in geography and mental models. Story thinking is a map and sensemaking pattern that supports macrocognition, which is based on the pattern of a story. And throughout this book we will look at several variations of this pattern, starting with the "half-pipe."

The Half-Pipe

Since we don't want to "reinvent the wheel" every day, we can "cut the story in half" and operate more efficiently in the bottom half of the story thinking cycle. As "mental misers," we work reactively within Automation until some Disruption occurs that makes us "look up" the trusted answer in Affirmation. If this works, then we don't have to go "over the top" to figure it out. Those readers familiar with snowboarding will recognize the "half-pipe" shape (see figure 1.3).

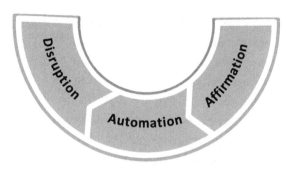

Figure 1.3—The Half-Pipe

We generally stay in the "half-pipe" for most things, which is OK since we aren't expected to understand the details of every topic. For example, when the electricity goes off (Disruption), I call the electric company. It usually tells me the lights should be back on shortly, and I trust the company to do its job (Affirmation). And when the power comes on, I'm back in business (Automation). I'm not expected to go out and investigate the problem (Investigation), come up with a solution (Ideation), and work on developing and implementing it (Expectation).

Staying down in the "half-pipe" allows us to work smart instead of working hard. It lets us operate in a team by trusting others to know how to do their job, so we can focus on our job. The downside occurs when we allow our thinking to become *stuck* in the half-pipe. Have you ever heard a discussion between two people trying to solve a problem, but both stuck in the half-pipe? It sounds something like this:

Julie: It's not working.

Joe: Well, did you try the other way I told you?

Julie: Yeah, that didn't work either.

Joe: Well, did you read the manual?

Julie: Yeah, I don't think this problem is in there.

Joe: Well, did you call the help desk?

Julie: Yeah, they said they should get back to me tomorrow.

Joe: Well, I guess you've done all you can do.

Julie: Yeah, I might as well go home.

Joe: Well, I'll see you tomorrow.

As individuals, and organizations, it is possible to become *stuck* in the "half-pipe." One reason we become stuck down in the half-pipe is because it is like working against gravity; we tend to rest at the bottom, performing transactional routines instead of expending the energy needed for projects and transformational change. Another reason we become stuck in the half-pipe is because the training we received provided memorized knowledge and steps for the half-pipe but not any thinking or problem-solving skills related to full-cycle learning within story thinking. The question is not if half-pipe thinking is good or bad, but about how we *balance* the two.

Balanced Thinking

Transformational change is driven by transformational thinking, which is when the underlying model or paradigm changes for how we think about what we are doing. In many companies today, this is represented by their annual release of a new product. *Transactional* change is driven by transactional thinking, which is repetitive and looks fairly the same each time. In many companies today, this is represented by the answers they provide to questions about their product or service. Workers today must do both—balancing our time between change that is transformational and change that is transactional (see table 1.1).

Transformational Change	Transactional Change
Full-Cycle of Story Thinking	Half-Pipe of Story Thinking
Stories and Projects	Routines and Status Quo
Innovation and Creativity	Productivity and Compliance
Thinking Slow	Thinking Fast
Transformational Leadership	Transactional Leadership
R&D Department	Operations Department

Table 1.1—Transformational Change vs. Transactional Change

In relationship to psychology, using Daniel Kahneman's (2011) terms, you can think of Full-Cycle navigation as "Thinking Slow" and think of Half-Pipe navigation as "Thinking Fast." In relationship to leadership, you can think of Full-Cycle navigation as "Transformational Leadership" and think of Half-Pipe navigation as "Transactional Leadership" (Bass, 1990). In relationship to an organization chart, you can think of Full-Cycle navigation as "R&D" (Research & Development) and think of Half-Pipe navigation as "Operations."

Imagine working in an organization where your entire career would allow you to focus on one or the other—transformational change or transactional change. A typical 1950's organization chart would represent not just two major types of work, but these two major types of change (see figure 1.4).

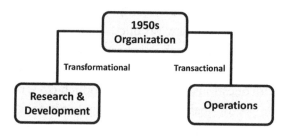

Figure 1.4—1950s Organization Chart

When thinking about the workforce of the future, with a clearly defined learning environment, we forget that many organizations in the past already had this, with a top-level organization structure that aligned to our fundamental types of change and thinking: R&D and Operations. Today, as we are expected to balance transformational and transactional work, the modern organization chart does not help us visualize the thinking within the work. But story thinking provides this visualization with the full-cycle required for transformational change, and the half-pipe required for transactional change.

The need to balance the two types of change goes beyond simply allocating *time* for both. Leading successful *transformational* change requires an understanding of how you will "land" in the half-pipe with new routines and *transactional* operations that can be maintained. The transformation will not become the new normal until basic controls are established, and key processes are codified to "lock in" productivity towards the desired individual routines and organizational culture.

In the past, maintaining the half-pipe's transactional capabilities required planning efforts to identify risks, and then create countermeasures ahead of time to attempt to *"sustain"* the current operational state. Predicting possible risks (disruptions) requires an ability to expect the unexpected. But now, the organization is too complex to predict everything that can happen to the current operational state. So, in addition to preparing and reacting to risks in the half-pipe, we find the term *"sustainability"* related to both types of change. Sustainability includes requirements for how quickly we can also move through the full-cycle to adapt to unplanned situations with minimal decision cycle times. Story thinking supports sustainability when it becomes the shared visualization of *change* for the entire leadership team.

Advancing Intelligence

One of the largest transformational changes that organizations are currently facing is called the Fourth Industrial Revolution (Schwab, 2017). The first industrial revolution was based on *steam* and mechanical production. The second revolution was based on *electricity* and assembly lines. The third revolution was based on *computing* and online workflow. All three of these technological advancements completely changed the underlying approaches towards business. But the next revolution will be even more profound. The fourth revolution is primarily based on *intelligence* and digital connectivity. Instead of just *using* steam or electricity or computers to perform business, and in addition to just *using* artificial intelligence to perform business—we will now be *competing* with artificial intelligence in the workplace. In the third revolution, while repetitive jobs were lost due to computing efficiency, equally new jobs were created to program and manage the computers. But in the intelligence revolution, the AI can write its own code. The impact of this coming revolution cannot be overstated given that our current education system has not even caught up to the requirements of the last revolution. With a workforce primarily trained to function in the half-pipe, and the robots and AI moving in to do those jobs, a perfect storm is coming.

During the 2018 SXSW Conference, Elon Musk said, "AI is far more dangerous than nukes." He said to reduce our risks, we need to ensure that advancements are "symbiotic with humanity." One of the reasons there is a growing fear of AI is due to how it operates from game theory. Some fear that the "end of game" state within the main program loop might not be reached by AI until catastrophic harm occurs for humans. But imagine the main program loop for AI based on story thinking, where there is no real end because one cycle leads into another, and balanced optimization is the goal rather than the simple construct of "win or lose." The "supervised" AI learning could align with half-pipe navigation, and the "unsupervised" AI learning could align with full-cycle navigation. Applying story thinking to AI thinking is one way to help AI become "symbiotic with humanity."

Just as AI will need to advance to become "symbiotic with humanity," the workforce of the future will require humans to advance to become "symbiotic with AI." Throughout history, there has been a fairly steady ratio between the required population of innovators and strategists (~30% full-cycle work) versus the population of labor workers (~70% half-pipe work). We see this ratio in "white-collar vs. blue-collar" jobs, "officer vs. enlisted" jobs, and organizational positions found in "R&D vs. Operations." In seeking labor (half-pipe) workers, there has always been cheap labor or offshore labor—but it has always included humans. Now, with the workforce including more AI, robots, and robotic process automation, the fundamental ratio of required job types is already changing—and will likely become *inverted*. With previous industrial revolutions, displaced half-pipe workers would be retrained for a new type of half-pipe job. But now, displaced half-pipe workers will need to be prepared to work in a full-cycle job.

The future of work is more than just humans working *with* intelligent technology; it will also require humans distinguishing themselves *from* the intelligent technology—and this means we will need more full-cycle thinkers. So, instead of viewing the fourth industrial revolution as a problem, what if we view it as an opportunity? We are born as learners—full-cycle learners. Humans will never become self-actualized by working in a repetitive, non-creative job. The fourth industrial revolution could be a growth opportunity for the individual as well as the organization.

In creating the workforce of the future, the focus is not on *knowledge* alone, since an organization's knowledge "is of less significance than are the processes needed to continuously revise or create knowledge" (Dixon, 1999). Embedding full-cycle thinking into the organization will mean replacing some models from the first and second industrial revolutions, that underlie business and education, with the sensemaking structure of story thinking. We will need smarter workers and smarter organizations. We will need smarter decisions from leaders with smarter ways to provide transparency. And we will need to rethink our common views of *change*, *learning*, and *leadership*. In essence, we will need… the rest of this book.

Your Turn

Picture the story thinking cycle as you work through the tasks below:

- Identify the last crisis in your organization that required rethinking how work is done, then describe the steps taken within each of the six story thinking phases.
- What information helps you anticipate the next crisis in your organization?
- Name a task or routine at work that should be redesigned by moving out of the half-pipe to perform full-cycle thinking.
- Identify the key change models used by your organization (see the appendix for examples).
- Determine if your organization looks for quick one-off workaround solutions (half-pipe) instead of stopping to rethink it (full-cycle).

- Create a plan to help half-pipe workers to become full-cycle workers in your organization, allowing for time and tools within Investigation, Ideation, and Expectation.

2

Changing Mindsets

"This is why I speak to them in parables, because seeing they do not see, and hearing they do not hear, nor do they understand." — Matthew 13:13

Q: What is the thinking behind story thinking?

The Inside Story

If a leader is not leading change, then what are they leading? When I ask this question of people in leadership positions, they recognize that the answer must be "change." And then they usually immediately realize that they do not know enough about *change* itself to call themselves an effective leader of transformational change. Leading change requires understanding change.

The story thinking cycle is more than just a list of six phases, where one might ask if there are possibly seven phases instead of six. There are underlying mindsets and mental states working inside the story, which are *producing* the six phases (Lewis, 2014). Understanding the underlying mindsets will provide deeper insights into the process of change, the mindset preferences that exist, and how to lead change more effectively. Below is the story thinking cycle with the underlying mindsets which produce the six phases (see figure 2.1).

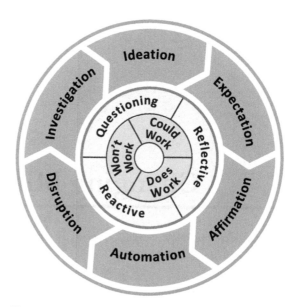

Figure 2.1—Mindsets Inside the Story Thinking Cycle

Notice in the graphic above the relationship between each phase and the underlying mindset:

- The **Automation** phase is produced from "Does Work / Reactive" beliefs.
- The **Disruption** phase is produced from "Won't Work / Reactive" beliefs.
- The **Investigation** phase is produced from "Won't Work / Questioning" beliefs.
- The **Ideation** phase is produced from "Could Work / Questioning" beliefs.
- The **Expectation** phase is produced from "Could Work / Reflective" beliefs.
- The **Affirmation** phase is produced from "Does Work / Reflective" beliefs.

In the rest of this chapter, we will look at the underlying mindsets in more detail, known as "workability beliefs" and "response modes."

Workability Beliefs

At the core of the story thinking cycle we find the fundamental beliefs related to our perception and definition of "working." You may have heard that "it either works or it doesn't work," but there is a third workability belief called *Could Work*, the mental place of most projects (see figure 2.2).

Figure 2.2—Workability Beliefs

Working is sometimes defined as including a certain amount of loss, waste, harm, relearning, or even failure. For example, the laws that govern our roads are considered to be working by most people, yet every day we find that there are accidents and people are killed. Our fundamental disputes are not about how to *solve* for something that won't work, but rather about the *definition* of workability. For most people, the way that it works today is based on the belief that it works and will continue to work—regardless of any of the known ongoing issues. But change leaders see things differently than most people. Instead of living with the issues found in the belief that this is the way it works, the change leader declares that it will no longer work. Transformational change starts when we move our belief from Does Work to Won't Work.

When Candy Lightner's daughter was killed by a drunk driver, she formed the organization called MADD (Mothers Against Drunk Driving) to get drunk drivers off the road. More than just changing laws, she changed the public perception of the difference between an accident, which has little accountability, and vehicular homicide, which does. She changed the status quo by changing our definition of Does Work so that it no longer includes deaths due to drunk driving. Today, her name and her story may be forgotten, as we are left just with the knowledge that it is against the law to drink and drive. And this is the nature of the story thinking cycle, where a new status quo eventually forgets the old status quo, as well as the process required for the change.

Within business, change leaders set the wheels of change in motion because they motivate people to discontinue accepting the status quo as "working." A change leader can work at the grass roots level or be viewed as a top-tier visionary leader. The key is that to effectively drive change, it takes more than just an authoritative reason. It requires changing the workability beliefs from Does Work to Won't Work, then from Won't Work to Could Work, and finally with a new solution, from Could Work to Does Work. As Klaus Schwab says in his book, *The Fourth Industrial Revolution*, "it is a leader's ability to continually learn, adapt and challenge his or her own conceptual and operating models of success that will distinguish the next generation of successful business leaders."

Does Not vs. Will Not Work

I have presented this model within academic, business, and leadership settings for almost a decade, with extremely positive comments and reviews. The one place where a minority of people have had difficulty is with the term "won't work." Some tell me that this model would make more sense to them if it said: "doesn't work" instead of "won't work." I have come to realize that there are personality predispositions for how we look at this. Are you a "doesn't work" person or a "won't work" person?

The problem with using "doesn't work" is that if it is still *working,* even *barely,* then you can't say that it *doesn't* work. Sometimes we wait too long to declare something as broken, making the fix more difficult and maybe impossible. With this mindset, we are willing to narrow our definitions each day for what "does" work. It works, but at what cost? It works, but for how much longer? We eventually find ourselves able to stay away from "doesn't work" beliefs only by narrowing our "does work" definition to: "it works for me today." And by this time, we may have run out of options and time to begin to make needed corrections towards "does work."

Sustainability is the concept at the core of the three workability beliefs. A sustainability mindset is asking if it works—and if it will *continue* to work. This mindset is at play, regardless if the topic is a computer, car, career, country, or civilization. The key question for a leader of change is if it will *continue* to work, given our ability to project into the future and identify risks. In the field of systems thinking, we know that some effects are far removed from their cause. This requires an ability to envision a probable future, which is related to the eternal questions of *now* versus *later* and is something that distinguishes humans from other animals. A good change leader responds to erosion, instead of just reacting to collapse. If you find that you are currently a Doesn't Work person, continue asking how long you can expect for the current state to continue working and you *may* begin to transform into a Won't Work person.

If "sustainability" is what defines a "won't work" person, then it is "justification" which defines a "doesn't work" person. In his book, *Sensemaking in Organizations*, Karl Weick refers to *justification* as "retrospective sensemaking," where the framework for sensemaking is in place but the *order* is based on earlier thoughts or actions instead of current observations. In their book, *The Enigma of Reason*, authors Mercier and Sperber expand on an earlier "justification hypothesis" and propose that we have *evolved* to reason for the sake of justifying our reactive nature, since we are "fundamentally biased and mentally lazy." For me, the correctness of the evolutionary theory, for how we got to this point, does not matter as much as the current beliefs that humans have, which manifest into either favoring sustainability or justification. A "doesn't work" person can always find a way to rationalize that the situation still *does* work, meaning they never have to actually accept the "doesn't work" belief.

There are some who are simply "mentally lazy" and favor justification. But there are many people who favor sustainability while still being "mental misers," meaning the disruption has to be great enough to overcome our tendency to remain in an automated state. If you are a change leader, this need to overcome the tendency of mental misers is a fundamental concept towards your success. This is why there are change models that tell us to start by creating a sense of urgency, or a burning platform. When attempting to change mindsets, a mentally lazy person will resist change for illogical reasons, whereas a mental miser may resist change for very logical reasons which need to be addressed.

Response Modes

Have you ever noticed that there are some similarities with most of the world's languages? While the words and letters look different, many languages *end* each sentence with either a question mark, a period, or an exclamation point. These are the specific ways that we respond mentally to our workability beliefs: Questioning, Reflective, and Reactive (see figure 2.3). We are either asking a question, and we communicate this using a question mark (?); or we are making a reflective statement, and we communicate this using a period (.); or we are making an emphatic reactive statement with conviction, and we communicate this using an exclamation point (!). In the Spanish language, acknowledging and communicating these three modes of the mind is so important that we also find clues at the *beginning* of each sentence: the inverted question mark (¿) initiates each question, and the inverted exclamation point (¡) initiates each reactive statement.

Figure 2.3—Response Modes

Response modes are not about what you are thinking; they are about what you are thinking *from*. For example, when the mom was asked why she dropped her kids off at school every day, she could have responded *reactively* that "this is the morning routine!" Or she could have responded by questioning with "why do you want to know??" But instead, she responded *reflectively* that she "is putting her faith in that school system." Working deliberately with intention is not the same as working reactively in routine. Being aware that our actions tend to settle into a reactive nature over time, it takes effort to remain intentional and reflective in the way that we respond to people and situations.

Asking powerful questions is a key way to promote learning and share knowledge. But it is important to recognize the difference between "questioning" versus a "mere question." The first clue, when using a written language, is that *questioning* tends to use more question marks than *mere questions* ("What???"). When using a verbal language, you may detect the difference in the tone, with more attitude found within questioning. A mere question is asked to gain information *within* the underlying model or assumption. But questioning comes from doubt *about* the underlying model or assumption. Consider the difference between, "Can you tell me how to do this?" versus "Are you sure you know how to do this??" Being aware of the difference between mere questions and questioning can help learning by challenging the underlying assumptions—which is required for *powerful* questions. A powerful question forces us to look at what we are thinking *from*, instead of just what we are thinking. And whether we realize it or not, we are all thinking from *story* thinking.

Emotional Tension

Our *change* beliefs are not only connected as we move *around* the story thinking cycle, they are also connected by the emotional tension found *inside* the cycle between opposite phases. In his book, *Good to Great*, Jim Collins says that one of the key elements of greatness is found in how we deal with life's challenges. His recommendation was not that we just learn more quickly, but that we reach an ability to *balance* our thinking between "working on vision" and "working in reality" at the same time. Successful people are able to "retain faith" and also "confront reality" without getting stuck in just one place.

Imagine a firefighter in a burning house, moving towards a person that has been overcome with smoke inhalation. He expects to reach the victim in time, before the fire consumes the building. But "at the same time" the firefighter realizes that his oxygen tank is almost empty. What would you do? This is known as "the hard choice" and the "hero's dilemma." Yet while most of us do not consider ourselves to be a hero, we do face these types of choices where our dreams and goals are just out of reach when we are confronted with today's reality, which forces us to make a hard choice. We know that it could work, and we are almost there—and at the same time, it appears that it won't work because at least for now a higher priority disruption may stop us. In terms of the story thinking cycle, will Expectation reach Affirmation before Automation reaches Disruption? Will we reach our long-term goal before our daily commitments make it impossible? These are the questions that come from emotional tension (see figure 2.4).

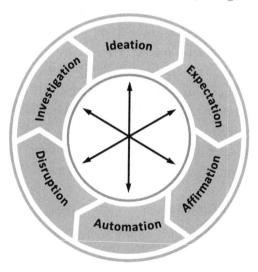

Figure 2.4—Emotional Tension

Current truths are always in tension with future aspirations. This emotional tension should be managed to ensure we don't get stuck in the half-pipe, giving up on our dreams. Asking the right questions will help us create the right tension between each of the three opposite pairs of phases within the story thinking cycle:

- Affirmation vs. Investigation
- Automation vs. Ideation
- Disruption vs. Expectation

Affirmation vs. Investigation: Is it possible that what we currently know is obsolete? Is it possible that there could be a higher truth? Healthy emotional tension requires that we *see what is true*, and at the same time, *seek a higher truth*. We need to remember our convictions but also remain truth-seeking.

Automation vs. Ideation: Is it possible that our current routine could be better? Is it possible that external forces could require us to change? Healthy emotional tension requires that we *see what is*, and at the same time, *seek what can be*. We need to keep our feet on the ground but also reach for the stars.

Disruption vs. Expectation: Is it possible that success will come before disaster if we work faster? Is it possible to abandon our dream for now and still be able to achieve it sometime in the future? Healthy emotional tension requires that we *see the problem*, and at the same time, *seek the promise*. We need to prepare for the worst but also expect the best.

In his book, *The Fifth Discipline: The Art & Practice of The Learning Organization*, Peter Senge tells us that "escaping emotional tension is easy—the only price we pay is abandoning what we truly want, our vision." Within the story thinking cycle, if we want to live a "half-pipe life," where there is no dream or hope of going "over the top," only the drudgery of everyday work, then we just need to free ourselves from emotional tension. Senge says that "truly creative people use the gap between vision and current reality to *generate* energy for change."

Instead of trying to escape emotional tension, as individuals and organizations, we should acknowledge it as part of story thinking and begin to *leverage* it. Instead of trying to have *zero* tension within the organization, the goal should be around *generating* energy by managing emotional tension. The strategy behind a collaborative ecosystem should be making sure that there is *healthy* tension between groups, where the tension is not personal and represents all three of the tensions described above.

Your Turn

Picture the story thinking workability beliefs and response modes as you work through the tasks below:

- Would you say that you tend to operate primarily from Does Work, Won't Work, or Could Work?
- Think about the decisions you have recently made and determine if they were primarily based on the past or the future.
- Are you able to perform questioning without confrontation, by not making it personal?
- Describe a crisis in the past where the majority agreed the current situation "Won't Work," and a new "Does Work" situation was formed.
- Describe the emotional tension your organization is experiencing right now.
- To begin creating healthy tension within your organization, identify the person or group that is best representing each of the six phases. Consider their attitude per phase:
  o **Disruption:** "Why do they keep deploying projects without preparing for the obvious risks?"
  o **Investigation:** "Why do they keep launching new projects without understanding root causes?"
  o **Ideation:** "Why do they keep resisting change, when some of my ideas are actually brilliant?"
  o **Expectation:** "Why do they keep adding features, when we are already out of time?"

- o **Affirmation**: "Why do they keep guessing and testing, when we have evidence-based facts?"
- o **Automation**: "Why do they keep making changes to what is working, when I have work to do?"

3

Continuous Improvement

"Change is the only constant in life." — Heraclitus

Q: What are some proven steps for continuous improvement which align with story thinking?

Establishing a Mission and Vision

A typical book related to transformational change and continuous improvement will tell us to start by writing down a mission statement and a vision statement. And there is a good reason for this, as it forces us to define a mission for who we are and why we exist, and a vision for what we are building and where we are going. This act of declaration is powerful and needed to bring clarity at the beginning of our strategic planning. The problem is that sometimes change consultants visualize their project as a straight line, with dates next to key events, and a stopping point for the end of the project. This representation of change diminishes the exercise of creating a mission and vision statement, because change is best represented as a cycle (see figure 3.1).

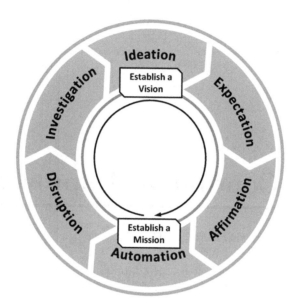

Figure 3.1—The Mission and Vision

A globe is a truer representation of the size and location of land masses on Earth than a 2-dimensional map, which shows distortions when the 3-dimensional globe is flattened. Similarly, our common view of *change* as a process line is a distortion of the actual mental activities being performed, which are cyclic and agile, not linear. As this relates to our mission statement, it means that we cannot use terms like "current state" and "future state" without seeing that the status quo position we seek is the place we already occupy. Our mission, for who we are and why we exist, is intricately linked to our identity as well as our daily behavioral routines.

With a cyclic view of change, we now understand that our well-defined mission statement can not only help *push* us into our desired future state, it can *pull* us there by simply declaring who we are—which has an immediate impact on daily values, beliefs, and routines that will be needed to reach our vision. You can't easily push a string—it is easier to pull a string. Effective life coaches understand this phenomenon and use events like "fire walking" (walking barefoot over hot coals) to bring about immediate change in how people see themselves, in what they are capable of doing which they previously thought impossible, and how to operate "now" in a way that will help to *pull* their vision into existence.

A factory mentality tells us that the way to create something new is to go through a linear process. But it doesn't work this way for people or organizations. There is a "quantum leap" that we can immediately take that will be needed to completely fulfill our vision. Leadership guru, John C. Maxwell said, "The secret of your success is determined by your daily agenda." There is a reason why dating experts say, "To find the right person, you must first BE the right person." So, after completing your vision and mission statement, before launching into a long journey towards the vision, there is a question we should answer about our mission: What are you going to do differently and routinely now that the mission statement is defined for who you are, so that the vision can be pulled into reality?

Managing the Story Cycle

People resist change—or so we are told. If I told you I would like to give you the winning Lottery ticket, would you decline? Would you say, "This would just be too much change"? Probably not. Why? Because the medical field has found that people don't resist change—they resist loss of control (Anderson, 1987). This is the interesting result from several studies on people with pre-surgical anxiety. Providing sensemaking information about the process one is about to go through reduces anxiety and resistance.

Is it possible that some change projects fail because they were based on a bad idea (yes)? Is it possible that some people resist change, not because they are resistant to change, but because they resist bad ideas (yes)? When the change leader can only describe the *change* and not the *improvement*, then the problem is not resistance to change. I acknowledge there are exceptions, but I believe the rule that "there are no bad students, only bad teachers." Similarly, I believe "there are no bad change resisters, only bad change leaders." Sometimes, the person identified as a "change resister" has vital information that will determine the ultimate success of the intended change. By having a "Collaboration" plan instead of just a "Communication" plan, we can provide sensemaking information into the process to reduce anxiety and gain valuable information from stakeholders. And a collaboration plan starts with a shared mental model and visualization of the overall process of change (see figure 3.2).

To provide insight and guidance into the change process, most change leaders acknowledge that a Strategic Plan is needed to identify the mission and the vision. A more-developed plan would also include identifying a monitoring process to ensure feedback into the plan; a SWOT analysis to identify our strengths, weaknesses, opportunities, and threats; a SOAR analysis based on *appreciative inquiry* to identify our strengths, opportunities, aspirations, and results expected; some guiding principles for how we will operate; and the high-level goals which will need to be met to achieve our vision. But we don't always approach new work with a new strategic plan, as Klaus Schwab says in his book, *The Fourth Industrial Revolution*, "strategic planning is being challenged by the need for companies to operate faster and with greater agility."

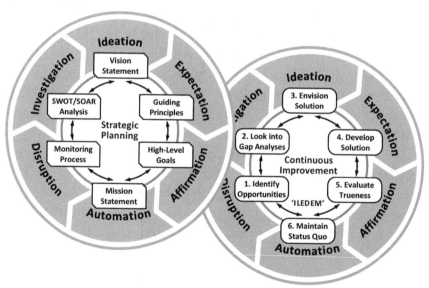

Figure 3.2—Strategic Planning vs. Continuous Improvement

Beyond a description of strategic planning, how do you visualize the roles of change management and project management? The levels of thinking involved (which I visualize as a pancake stack of story thinking cycles), includes the concept of strategic planning, followed by the concept of continuous improvement, which can be incremental or transformational. From here, depending on the type of changes required, the picture continues with the discipline of change management, the discipline of project management, and the discipline of human performance improvement, etc. I believe that change leaders create anxiety and resistance to change when they skip the concept of continuous improvement and begin their communication plans with the action steps related to their discipline (see the appendix for comparing these disciplines with story thinking). In an organization with a learning environment, the concept of continuous improvement will still be in place, even after the "change" professionals have left.

When we consider how to move organizations through a cycle of continuous improvement, the steps taken should directly align with the sensemaking pattern of the story thinking cycle. The problem with traditional change management is that the focus has been on the "roll-out" of the change (steps 4-6 above), with an emphasis on communication, training, and how to deal with resistance to change. With *strategic* change management, the focus is on the entire story thinking cycle (steps 1-6 above). Given that story thinking is about applied sensemaking, not just memorization, notice that the six steps for successful continuous improvement are based on best practices for each phase of the story cycle. The change method we will be covering in this chapter is one I created, called ILEDEM ("I led 'em"), which is a mnemonic that represents the first letter of each step within continuous improvement:

- Step 1 (*Identify Opportunities*) is for the Disruption phase.
- Step 2 (*Look into Gap Analyses*) is for the Investigation phase.
- Step 3 (*Envision Solution*) is for the Ideation phase.
- Step 4 (*Develop Solution*) is for the Expectation phase.
- Step 5 (*Evaluate Trueness*) is for the Affirmation phase.
- Step 6 (*Maintain Status Quo*) is for the Automation phase.

Notice also that the six steps are shown as an *agile* (iterative) methodology, with the arrows moving in both directions, instead of a linear approach. An agile navigation through the story thinking cycle means that we may rock between phases before moving forward through the story. For example, an investigation may likely tell us more about the situation than when it was first defined as a disruption, leading us to redefine and reprioritize the issue. During Ideation, a particular design may require us to go back and reinvestigate before settling on a final design. And the evaluation of a pilot program may require going back for additional development towards a production implementation.

Some organizations, especially familiar and highly functional teams, may appear at first to have a chaotic nature when watching them work together. But in reality, they have a highly agile nature to their decision-making processes, which, if successful, still adhere to the overall principles of agile navigation while ultimately moving around the story thinking cycle. In the rest of this chapter, we will view each of the six steps in more detail, but keep in mind that each step can be reached in a sequential or agile manner.

Step 1: Identify Opportunities

When something out of the ordinary occurs, how do you normally react? The first step towards successful continuous improvement is properly identifying the disruption. A disruption is simply a situation or idea that is out of the ordinary, which could be a problem or an opportunity, which is how many innovations begin. But many people think of disruptions only as *problems*. In fact, the term "disruption" is used by many people as a *synonym* for "problem." This tends to make them shy away from a disruption instead of embracing it as a beginning point for positive change. To be a good change leader, we should be able to take this a step further and find ways to *initiate* the disruption, thereby *becoming* the catalyst of change. Yet, without a good understanding of disruptions, as both problems and opportunities, I have seen people get "stuck on step 1" instead of being able to continue around the story thinking cycle.

"Identifying opportunities" is not about *dismissing* the problem, it is about not *dwelling* on the problem. It is important to appreciate the problem, but also to appreciate the opportunity. To help us properly identify problems and opportunities, the 20 Disruption Archetypes are presented below (see table 3.1).

Problems	Opportunities
Emergency/Crisis (Immediate Action Required)	**Window of Opportunity** (Timeframe to Seize)
Issue (Limitation, Obstacle)	**Growth Opportunity** (Feature, Stepping Stone)
Non-issue (False Alarm, Distraction, Trivial)	**Blessing in Disguise** (Problem turned Opportunity)
Risk (Possibility of Future Issue)	**Proactivity** (Predict, Prevent, Prepare, Preempt)
Temptation (False Sign of Fortunate Disruption)	**Incentive** (True Sign of Fortunate Disruption)
Downside (Negative Aspect, Known Tradeoff)	**Upside** (Positive Aspect, Advantage)
Downward Spiral (Decline, Creeping Normality)	**Upward Spiral** (Momentum, Compound Interest)
Ending (Boiling Frog, Termination)	**Beginning** (Leapfrog, Transformation)
Criticism (Provokes Defensiveness)	**Constructive Feedback** (Promotes Growth)
Pessimist (Becoming Part of the Problem)	**Optimist** (Becoming Part of the Opportunity)

Table 3.1—20 Disruption Archetypes

Notice that for each type of *problem* that we may encounter, there is another way to look at it through the lens of an *opportunity*. This immediately alters our emotional connection to the situation and changes the way we approach the rest of the phases in the story thinking cycle. In cases where the problem cannot entirely be viewed as an opportunity, at least seeing both a problem *and* opportunity allows us to have a balanced emotional approach. Let's look at some examples from the table above:

Emergency: An emergency is a problem that requires immediate action, yet still could be viewed as a "window of opportunity" with positive emotions. Even within an ambulance on the way to the hospital, there is more than just panic—there is hope of arriving in time. Every child that has ever heard the sound of an ice-cream truck coming through the neighborhood knows what a "window of opportunity" is. While this idea can be applied to topics as complex as rockets, with the concept of a "launch window," it still applies to everyday events that we can choose to ignore, react to as a problem, or seize as an opportunity. And when the disruption is our daily awakening from sleep, the Latin term "Carpe diem" applies as well: Seize the day. A window of opportunity is a great concept that includes both a sense of urgency and a positive emotion. It is the reason why Marketing departments make signs that say "50% Off – Today Only!" Imagine starting each day and each project with this same emotion.

Issue: Viewing an issue as a growth opportunity is difficult for most of us because it requires that we consider changing ourselves and not just our situation. Did your car just run into a pothole, causing untold problems in steering alignment and car repair bills? Or was that an opportunity to learn how to develop a smartphone app, as one entrepreneur decided, to help connect residents with their local government services? By seeing both a problem and opportunity, it allows us to respond to the problem while also seeing ways to grow from the experience.

Non-issue: I once had a smoke detector in my house that would automatically call the fire department when it thought the house was on fire. One day, the steam from cooking triggered the smoke detector and a fire truck was sitting outside my house. This was still a problem, but ultimately not an issue. However, it did make me research other options for protecting my house and I found a service that was better, and it cost less than the previous system. We all experience false alarms from time to time, and we are glad when the negative event turns out to be neutral. But it is also possible that the negative event can eventually turn into a positive event if we look for it—a blessing in disguise.

Risk: There is an adage based on negative thinking called "Murphy's Law" which states, "whatever can go wrong, will go wrong." Considering the risks and threats that apply to our projects and organizations, it is prudent to a point, to identify possible future issues in that it provides us the opportunity to think proactively about solutions. But beyond this purpose, only causes us to dwell on possible issues instead of real and possible opportunities. If we can use our imagination to identify risks, then we can also use our imagination to identify proactive ways to prove Mr. Murphy was wrong.

Temptation: A fishing lure is a device used as fishing bait, designed to attract the attention of a fish. It is designed specifically to look and move in a way that tricks a fish into temptation. The cheese sits in a mouse trap as a lure for the same purpose. The intended reaction is that the *temptation*, which is a *false* sign of a fortunate disruption, will be viewed as an *incentive*, which is a *true* sign of a fortunate disruption. Fortunately, humans are not as gullible as fish and mice. We are not lured by promotions, attracted to shiny objects, pressured by sale signs, or fooled by the word "Free!" Actually, as we all know, humans can be very trusting. Yet, at the same time, we can also find real incentives, even if in the face of temptation, where the incentive would be to keep moving.

Downside: There are two sides to every coin, and there are two sides to every situation—the upside and the downside—the positive view and the negative view. But it is more complicated than this because sometimes we need to find the upside *within* the downside. Sometimes there is a Known Tradeoff that should be considered before creating a sense of urgency and getting everyone spun-up about reacting to a disruption. For example, imagine you are a factory Supervisor and your company Vice President tells you that too many people are getting sent to the hospital. He says that safety is the main concern, even if it means slowing down the production line. This is a tradeoff decision that requires a leader to say "I would rather err on the side of X." But the problem in many organizations is that some time later, the same VP or someone else will complain that the production numbers have dropped, and they must be fixed immediately. In today's complex organizations, most decisions are tradeoff decisions, yet our organizations appear to suffer from schizophrenia when they react unwittingly to every downside, lurching the organization between competing priorities because the tradeoffs are forgotten.

Downward Spiral: Sometimes it seems like our problems are mounting and building on each other in a way that creates a downward spiral that is impossible to escape. In aviation, a plane can enter a tailspin which can be fatal if not corrected, and the interesting thing is that the correction for the pilot is counterintuitive. If what seems intuitive is not working, try something else. As we mentally view ourselves in a downward spiral it is important to mentally view transitioning to an upward spiral. Each day is an opportunity to find a way to change directions. When building a skyscraper, you first have to dig deep to ensure you are resting on solid ground. On a trampoline, if you want to jump higher you first have to drop lower. Maybe we are not on our way down. Maybe we are about to go higher.

Ending: Within a cycle, we know that the ending of one thing is the beginning of another. If one job has ended, another may be beginning. If one career has ended, another may be beginning. Compared to just a few decades ago, it is now common to go through several professional cycles. And each beginning has the opportunity to become a beautiful transformation. Imagine the caterpillar worried about its ending as it contemplates its situation within the silky cocoon. Then imagine it filled with wonder as it emerges as a butterfly. Sometimes, we may be struggling with the impact of termination when instead we could be gladly anticipating a transformation.

Criticism: Some would say that the biggest difference between *criticism* and *constructive feedback* is the way that they are communicated. Others would say that the biggest difference is in the way they are received. Constructive feedback is an opportunity to improve. When done correctly, we really don't thank our evaluator enough. Criticism goes beyond constructive feedback and is a problem because it becomes personal and usually based in faultfinding. But the key is remembering that it doesn't have to be *our* problem. I once took a graduate class where the teacher was extremely critical of other research and papers submitted by my classmates while introducing a new topic. When it was our turn to present an overview of any lesson we had learned in class, we each presented on the topic of constructive feedback, and how we, if we were the teacher, would have presented the new topic. The teacher sat silently while each student modeled professional constructive feedback, and I still passed the class.

Pessimist: Probably the worst type of disruption is when we allow ourselves to become part of the problem. When driving a car, there are many things that can go wrong, but the second that we panic, we just make everything that much worse. When it comes to how we view disruption, the problems only get bigger the second that we approach them as a pessimist. This is the sad turning point towards missing out on golden opportunities because we will just not see them, and some, we will push away. The *Power of Positive Thinking* (Peale, 2003) and approaching disruptions as an *optimist* has proven to be the best *Step 1*.

The 20 Disruption Archetypes show us that the term "disruption" is not a *synonym* for "problem." Seeing both a problem *and* opportunity allows us to have a balanced emotional approach, which will affect how we move through the rest of the cycle. Once we have identified the opportunities, and prioritized a complete list of disruptions, we are ready to enter into Step 2, to look into gap analyses.

Step 2: Look into Gap Analyses

Before we can look into gap analyses, we first need to define the gap, which is the performance difference between our current state and our desired state (see figure 3.3). In looking at our current state, it is helpful to consider both positive and negative aspects, instead of just negative. The way that we enter this step will have an impact on how we define our current state, and can also have an impact on how we leave this step. For example, if Disruption is essentially approached as a problem, then we will enter Investigation looking for an answer to what is wrong, or what went wrong, or who is to blame. And if Disruption is essentially approached as an opportunity, then we will enter Investigation looking for an answer to how something works, so that we can create something new with it in the Ideation phase.

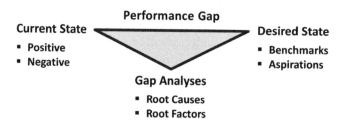

Figure 3.3—Gap Analyses

For example, when the right-front wheel stopped working on the Spirit Mars Rover, NASA could not just send out a pit crew to fix it. After NASA approached this disruption as a problem and investigated for a solution to this negative state, it was clear that the rover's driving days were over. But then NASA approached the disruption as an opportunity and considered the positive aspects of the current state for what was still working on the rover and what else it could still do. This led to a new idea: what if we drive the rover in reverse? And by driving backwards, with the stuck wheel dragging behind, it pushed away the top layer of Martian soil to reveal a new discovery: salt—which meant there was once water on Mars. The way that we *think* about our current state can affect our future state. The practice of *Appreciative Inquiry* is an important part of this step. In fulfilling your quest, the mindset of *appreciation* can be more powerful than a mindset of *problem-solving* (Cooperrider and Whitney, 2005).

The other side of the performance gap is the desired state, which can be a benchmark or an aspiration. A benchmark is just a standard or reference that has been established. If our current state is the problem that our car is broken, then usually our future state is the *benchmark* of our car in a working state. But, if our current state has some positive aspects which allow us to consider other options, then the future state could include the *aspiration* of getting a new car. Sometimes within a business, the benchmark is based on a known ability or "best practice" that other organizations already have. When we "benchmark" other organizations, it could be for the purpose of reaching their standard. But sometimes it is for the purpose of knowing the current "best practice" so that we can have the *aspiration* of going *beyond* the current standard. Sometimes, continuous improvement is not started by a problem, but just from the opportunity and aspiration to improve.

Once the performance gap is defined with a clear picture of the current and desired state, we can look into the gap analyses to understand the causes of the gap and main obstacles for closing the gap. In determining the root *causes*, there is a common practice of asking the question *why* five times—known as the "5-WHYs" method of getting at a root cause. For example: "(Why?) the death was caused by injuries, (Why?) caused by an accident, (Why?) caused by icy roads, (WHY?) caused by freezing rain, (WHY?) due to the low temperature." But was "low temperature" really the root cause? In some cases, the best explanation is not a single cause at the end of a linear causality chain. Sometimes the better explanation is from the root *factors*. So, I call this the "5-WHATs" method of getting at the key factors involved. For example: "the accident was due to inexperience, *combined* with night-driving and a rain-slick road, *combined* with poor windshield wipers, *combined* with not wearing a seatbelt."

In his book, *Apollo Root Cause Analysis*, Dean Gano ironically discusses the "myth" of the "root cause." He found that the commonly accepted practice called a "root cause analysis" is based on the false premise that there will be a "root cause." And when asking several people to define the root cause of an accident, you will get several different answers. So instead, he teaches people to focus on solving problems rather than finding blame, and that usually involves looking for multiple factors, not a single root cause. The "5-WHYs" method follows "Cause-Effect" thinking, while the "5-WHATs" method follows "Systems" thinking, which recognizes that there are usually multiple interconnections operating together, and the conditions of several root factors can create the "perfect storm" or "magic moment."

Another advantage of thinking in terms of "root factors" instead of finding a single "root cause" is that it forces us to consider the impact and interaction of many variables in the organization, from many directions. Some of those variables include job factors, performer factors, process factors, system factors, organizational factors, management factors, cultural factors, environment factors, customer factors, competition factors, etc. Within the field of Human Performance Improvement, the research indicates that we tend to focus on the *performer* as a key factor affecting poor performance, thereby attempting corrections with *training*, when it is usually one or more of the other factors that have much more influence into the situation than the individual performer (Stolovitch, 1992).

Step 3: Envision Solution

In Step 3, we envision a solution, as we operate within the Ideation phase of story thinking. As we saw in Chapter 2, this means that you are creatively questioning towards a solution that could work. The first type of questioning should be towards seeking the right questions to ask. Some call this "brainstorming questions" or "question storming." Unfortunately, we usually start with "brainstorming" for *ideas* related to a *predetermined* question. We even make sure there is no judgement for any of the ideas that people throw out at this point. But without first allowing for a diversity of questions for how to frame a solution, we inadvertently have limited the diversity of ideas that are generated. Seeking a diversity of initial questions and ideas represents the *opening* towards envisioning a solution. Equally important is the *closing* towards envisioning a solution. This means articulating your error preferences ("We would rather err on the side of safety over cost"), documenting tradeoff decisions in the selection process to provide transparency, and deciding on a design and plan that can be backed with enough capability and motivation within Step 4 to begin development. While we sometimes think about creativity just for the opening of ideation, we need creativity in both the opening *and* closing towards envisioning a solution.

According to a survey published in Businessweek (Kern, 2010), CEOs now value one leadership competency above all others: *creativity*. To pull out of the economic downturn, the focus is not on operational effectiveness, influence, or some other common leadership competency. Instead, the focus is on innovation and the leaders that can disrupt the status quo.

Steve Jobs once said: "Creativity is just connecting things." So, is creativity just for some people or can we all be creative? Is there a pattern to the creation process that we can all use? I remember as a kid, my father would take me with him to the hardware store. As I looked at the aisles and aisles of lumber, tools, and other supplies, a model of this interaction came to me. I thought of this model as CLICK (see figure 3.4). I liked it because of the sound that it made, but mainly because it helped me make sense of what I was seeing:

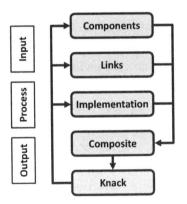

Figure 3.4—CLICK Model of Ideation

There were *Components* (lumber, bricks); *Links* (nails, concrete); *Implementations* (implements like hammers and shovels, and how-to books for the process of implementation); *Composites* (which were the new creations); and *Knacks* (the capability of the composite to be used for some larger model of CLICK). Boards become walls, walls become houses, and houses become communities.

This is a model that is also seen *outside* the hardware store, in other domains, including ideas of the mind. The questioning for ideation is either going to set the mind to ask what others *have* done (derivation) or ask what *can* be done (innovation), and this is the path to what has *never* been done (unique innovation). I've been in ideation meetings that start with this question: "What features do our competitors have that we don't, and how fast can we get them?" It would be one thing if questions like this were balanced with questions for real innovation. But when it becomes apparent that these are the *only* questions that you are able to ask, you know you will never see real innovation from that organization. Let's look at the CLICK model in more detail:

Components: Sid Caesar is quoted as saying, "The guy who invented the wheel was an idiot. The guy who invented the other three, he was a genius." I can't think of a better way to illustrate the CLICK model. Take a look today at everything you see one of and imagine if there were two, or four, or a hundred of them. If you have ever used a computer with two monitors, it is hard to go back to just one. Imagine looking at a math book that shows how to "triangulate" your position between three radio towers—then designing the constellation of GPS satellites. Innovation can start with what is right in front of you.

Links: Links are the nails between boards; the concrete between bricks; and the glue between paper—and ideas. Make a list of the links you find today: tape, paperclips, rope, and staples. But get creative: gravity, transitions in TV news stories, and links in a chain, which are also components. This is how ideas work: one idea turns into a link for another idea. For the product you would like to improve, what are the links that hold the components together? What if there were less links? Would it be easier to manufacture?

Implementation: Sometimes, it's not what you make, but how you make it, that makes the difference. From the ramps that built the Great Pyramids, to Leonardo da Vinci's method to pour bronze for his statue of a horse—implements and implementation are the "hidden how" of ideation. The idea that implementation is a key to innovation is what drives companies to try to get patents on their processes. See how many implements you can find today. Some people just call them tools. But some implements are used again, some are thrown away, and some are left inside the composite. What would your implementation process look like if some steps were performed by robots and others by humans?

Composite: We are constantly building something, with components, links, implements, and implementations. And this is the new composite that we give a name to; usually based on the purpose (knack) we had in mind. Try to find things today that could be used as a component, link, or implement of something else. Does it solve a problem? Or, imagine *starting* here and working backwards within CLICK to see what it would take to make what you can imagine.

Knack: Marketing and Psychology Departments teach universal human needs and Maslow's "hierarchy of needs"—the foundations of problems which we expect innovation to solve. Yet we teach science and technology from the standpoint of "how," which is why technology education by itself fails as a stand-alone solution for innovation. Imagine a list of human needs and positive emotions, like safety, belonging, and love. Imagine another list of innovation methods, like faster, better, cheaper, and easier. Now you have a table made from two lists. Find a cell that nobody else has worked in for your domain.

Innovation starts with being willing to go "over the top" and not stay in the "half-pipe" of the story thinking cycle. Disruption should be an opportunity and not just a problem. Investigation should be driven from questions that lead to exploration and not just inspection. And then, Ideation can be approached with questions that produce innovation, and hopefully uniqueness, instead of just derivations. While outsourcing tasks for automation can increase proficiency, some "core competency" needs to remain—and it needs to be tied to the tasks we are able to go "over the top" with. It is more difficult to outsource innovation than to outsource automation.

In his book, *A Whole New Mind*, Daniel H. Pink describes the current era of "left-brain" detail thinkers giving way to a new era of "right-brain" big picture thinkers (Pink, 2005). The next age will belong to those who think in terms of designs (not details), concepts (not processes), and innovation (not duplication). Now try your variations on the CLICK model, for example: simplify implementation

(Ford factory), add another component (2 PC monitors), remove a component (rimless eyeglasses), or embed an implement (tile spacers). The key is to continue to ask, "What if?" questions during the *opening*, and "Then what?" questions during the *closing* towards envisioning a solution.

Step 4: Develop Solution

In Step 4, we develop a solution, as we operate within the Expectation phase of story thinking. As we saw in Chapter 2, this means that you reflectively believe that your solution could work. Passive expectation is having *hope* that something could work. But active expectation is having *faith* that what you are *doing* could work. And many times, it is *active* expectation that is required to bring about the affirmation of change. To see an idea come to fruition, we may have to *do* something ourselves, rather than just hope that it will happen. And becoming active requires faith in something—like yourself, or an idea, or God, or another person. By simply driving down the road with the expectation of reaching my destination, it shows my faith in other drivers and their ability to stay on their side of the road. So "faith" is not a word associated uniquely with religion, but is a component of active expectation, regardless the affirmation that we seek. When Thomas Edison was trying thousands of combinations to produce a commercially successful light bulb, he was acting in the faith that the right combination would work and that he just needed to find it.

You are either like Thomas Edison, who could *reflectively* say what knowledge his faith rested upon as he worked in expectation of developing his light bulb—or you are like his less-knowledgeable assistant, stepping through instructions that allowed him to work in reactive automation, based on the trust he had in authority, his boss, Mr. Edison. In looking at a situation that is not working, one observer might say that the person has deep faith in his or her expectation, and yet another observer might say that the person is stubbornly facing constant disruption from blindly working in automation.

This built-in ability for a story cycle to have clean separations for each person on a team is why we see companies with separate departments for R&D and Operations—and is also how the government can perform complex missions while maintaining secrets with a "need to know" policy. Faith is what is not communicated. Trust is what is split to allow this to work. Mr. Edison's assistant trusts him, so there is not a need to fully know everything he knows that provides him with *faith* in his expectations. The assistant's job is not to understand everything that Thomas Edison understands. The assistant *trusts* Mr. Edison and is therefore able to simply work in the half-pipe.

When viewing *change* as a cycle instead of a process line, some have asked where the term "implement" or "roll-out" occurs. According to the Cambridge dictionary, the term "develop" means "to grow or cause to grow; to bring or come into existence." The agile navigation within this cycle means that we can expect to go back and forth several times between Step 4 (Expectation) and Step 5 (Affirmation), using several, if not all, of the seven stages of development (see table 3.2).

Stage	Stages of Development	Description
1	Picture of Concept	Think it (thought experiment)
2	Proof of Concept	Test it (verify idea)
3	Prototype	Try it (verify design)
4	Pilot	Try it on (on a trial basis)
5	Plunge	Take it (devote yourself fully)
6	Patch	Tweak it (course corrections)
7	Production	Trust it (abate evaluation)

Table 3.2—The 7 Stages of Development

Stage 1 is a thought experiment, where we "think it." Stage 2 is a proof of concept, where we "test it." Stage 3 is a prototype, where we "try it" to verify the design. Stage 4 is a pilot, where we "try it on" during a trial basis. Stage 5 is where we "take the plunge," and commit to it, which is usually the stage associated with implementation. Stage 6 is a patch, where we "tweak it" for minor corrections. And stage 7 is the production stage of development, where we "trust it" and know that others trust it without first testing it. So, the production stage can also be associated with implementation, but it happens as a half-pipe operation that has already been practiced several times.

As we view *change* as a cycle instead of a process line, we need to remember that we normally use agile navigation between phases. So, in addition to going back and forth between Step 4 (develop) and Step 5 (evaluate), depending on our success in development, we may need to go back to Step 3 to find another solution, or even go back to Step 2 to reconsider our underlying assumptions and analyses about our current and desired state.

Step 5: Evaluate Trueness

In Step 5, we evaluate what we have developed in Step 4, as we operate within the Affirmation phase of story thinking. As we saw in Chapter 2, this means that we no longer reflectively believe that our solution *could* work; we now believe that it *does* work. While there are many types of tests, based on the types of things and ideas we could be developing, at this point we ultimately want to know what we will trust as being *true*. It may be true that our prototype flying invention can actually fly, but it may be false that it is stable, or can fly for more than two minutes. It may be true that the software project launched on time, but it may be false that it works as advertised.

Also, it may be true that the overall project was successful, but it may be false that the team executed flawlessly. At this step in the cycle, in addition to evaluating the results, it is also critical to evaluate the process. Some teams document "lessons learned" at this step because it is the only way to promote continuous improvement of the process and team dynamics. Other teams perform an AAR (after-action review) which is a more structured debriefing to evaluate what worked and what could work better, and what is true and what is false about the capabilities of the process and team.

Being clear in our evaluations for what is true allows us to move from Step 4 to Step 5 with details that produce trust in the results, and continuous improvement in the processes. This will also allow us to reach the Affirmation phase in the half-pipe, when we just want to *cite* an answer that someone else has determined without having to "reinvent the wheel." So, when working in a learning environment, for Affirmation, we need to evaluate full-cycle results, but also make them findable, understandable, and trustable for citing in the half-pipe.

In evaluating *trueness*, the opinions on the team may differ. Some may believe that the idea worked (true) and others may think that it did *not* work (false). And for each of these beliefs (true/false), the results could actually be true, or actually be false. This produces four outcomes as shown in the "Reality Table" below (see table 3.3).

Decision / Belief	Reality of Truth	
	Actually True	**Actually False**
True	True Positive (Correct)	False Positive (Type I Error)
False	False Negative (Type II Error)	True Negative (Correct)

Table 3.3—Reality Table

The two ways that we can be correct, is to believe something is true when it is actually true and believe something is false when it is actually false. This means that there are two ways that we can be wrong, called a Type I Error and a Type II Error. An example of a Type I Error would be a false alarm, where we believe there is a fire because the fire detector is beeping, but it is actually broken and there is no fire. An example of a Type II Error would be where we believe there is *no* fire, maybe due to prior false alarms, yet the fire detector is working correctly. In the example of having a smoke detector going off, a Type II Error is a bigger problem than a Type I Error. A Type II Error would mean there is a fire and the detector is operating correctly, but you ignore it and believe everything is actually OK. Just remember that the warning sound signaling that there is a problem could also be coming from stakeholders or people on your team. So, consider the four, not two, options before responding.

For any idea which we accept as a fact without doubt, we are working within some reality table within the Affirmation phase of the story thinking cycle. The question then becomes one related to if it is a belief or decision, if that decision is still credible, and how the decision was formed. There is a big difference between using Affirmation just to *affirm* and *reaffirm* (using half-pipe thinking) versus using Affirmation to *confirm* and *disaffirm* (using full-cycle thinking). Did you *find* the answer, or did you *figure* it out? Did you use "social validation" or "scientific validation"? Documenting our "lessons learned" requires knowing *what* it true, and also *how* we know. And these answers can cascade. For example, I trust that the air pressure in my car's tires is correct because I know that I checked them, and I trust the air gauge on the pump because I know it was tested, because I trust the dated sticker on the pump, etc. Knowing the answer to truth testing is important, but so is the answer to how it was found.

Step 6: Maintain Status Quo

In Step 6, we maintain what we have evaluated in Step 5, as we operate within the Automation phase of story thinking. As we saw in Chapter 2, this is where the organization's reactive nature is aligned with what has been defined as "working." This is where we find "routine" in daily operations. And as the name implies, this is where some of our routine operations are moved to computers and robots so that operations are more proficient and predictable.

This final step in the cycle, bringing us back into a reactive state of Automation, can happen slowly over time as we fall into routine and forget exactly why we do what we do, or it can be planned to quickly bring us back to an efficient state for managing operational and maintenance activities. And instead of just planning to provide training, the planning can be built into our solutions. It was in one of these planning meetings that I realized there must be a structured way to think about how to plan out and control the maintaining of proficiency. We were designing the user interface for a new workflow software solution, and after an hour of discussing how the screen should appear, how the user would be prompted to enter specific information, how the training would need to be created, and how to check for input errors from the user, I finally asked if the information needed could be automatically pulled in so that the user would not need to do anything. We should have asked this question earlier.

Within any business operation, there are key questions that are asked to determine if proficiency is being obtained and maintained. The answer to each question will drive additional questions. To help facilitate these series of questions, I created the Proficiency Waterfall (see figure 3.5) to illustrate that whatever question is not managed at a higher level will "spill over" to the next level down.

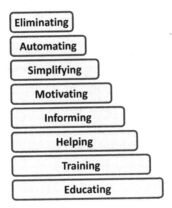

Figure 3.5—The Proficiency Waterfall

Since the goal within the Automation phase is to maintain a level of *proficiency*, the first questions should be around seeing if anything can be eliminated. This can be the first step in a project or part of an annual "spring cleaning." Whatever is not eliminated falls to the next set of questions designed around finding human actions that can be automated. If not automated, then find out how to simplify the work with a better organization design, process, template, or user interface. After simplifying the work, we are ready to involve workers by providing some motivation, assuming here that this should be all that is needed if the work is now intuitive. If not, then we can expect the workers to take the correct actions by informing them on what they should do. If this will not produce the desired effect, then there may be ways to help them *while* they are doing it. If that doesn't work, then there may need to be some training or education *before* they begin working. Why train people on a task that could be simplified or automated or even eliminated? So, let's look at each level of the Proficiency Waterfall in more detail:

Eliminating: Business guru, Peter Drucker, is quoted as saying, "There is nothing so useless as doing efficiently that which should not be done at all." At first it may be hard to imagine that work can simply be eliminated. But there are usually opportunities for elimination when you look through the tradeoff lens of costs versus benefits. There are many things that we may be "busy" doing that do not align with our core mission.

Automating: If we just take a paper-based process and place it online, we have simply "computerized" that process instead of creating a digital transformation. The point in having an online process is to take advantage of "artificial automation" as much as possible. And with the progressive advancements in AI, there are always more opportunities than the last time you checked. For example, let's say you run a hotel chain and want someone to scan in and read the thousands of handwritten complaint and compliment forms that come in. If you haven't been keeping up with technology, you might not realize that "text analytics" software can automatically read the text from all of the forms and summarize them for you.

Simplifying: The way that work is presented to us can usually be simplified at several levels. For example, undue complexity can be found within the organizational structure, the work processes, the provided templates, or the user interface. Simplifying a particular job can not only make the *current* workers more productive, it can entirely change *who* needs to do the job. Less-skilled or less-knowledgeable workers can sometimes do the job that previously required a highly skilled (highly paid) worker. When you continue simplifying to the point that the average consumer can perform the task, then you have changed the requirements to the degree that allows for self-help— where your customers and potential customers are doing the work. Just make sure nothing blows up. Before allowing gas station customers to pump the gas themselves, they installed a breakaway coupling on each hose, which allows us to drive off with a hose dragging behind us, instead of causing more damage. Designing a self-help system requires a lot of automating and simplifying to make it foolproof. But it also involves building in the reasons that someone would be motivated to use the system.

Motivating: Once, I was working with a team of trainers to help train a sales force on a new product. The sales team had already taken some basic training on the new product, but they were still selling the older product by a wide margin. Some thought they needed additional training to understand the new features to be able to start selling the newer product. But after a short evaluation of what the sales team currently understood, it was clear that they knew the new product quite well. They also knew the compensation structure very well. You see, the sales team knew that they made more from sales commissions when they sold the older product than when they sold the newer one. Getting the right operational performance is not just about technical knowledge—it includes the right motivation.

Informing: Sometimes I already know *how* to do it; I just didn't know that you *wanted* me to do it now. Tasks, updates, alerts, issues, and workarounds are some of the key ways that workers need to be informed to maintain the status quo. And "informing" is not just about media and sending e-mail; it is built into the user interface inside the apps that we use every day. The way that the online work is designed needs to be able to inform knowledge workers with enough information and clarity to be able to make the right operational decisions.

Helping: If simply informing me to perform a task doesn't work because I'm unsure or rusty about the task, that doesn't necessarily mean you need to send me off to a training class. In between "informing" and "training" is where we find "helping" on the Proficiency Waterfall. This is where I'm still performing a task, while being provided with some help. And if you are designing a self-help system for your customers, this is the last stop. You really can't expect to offer a day of training to your customers on how to use your poorly designed Web site. Helping can come in the form of talking to someone at a "help desk," or a paper "job aid" on the wall, or an elaborate Electronic Performance Support System (EPSS). Given that we don't remember most of what we learned in a training class, "helping" strategies can be a big *help* in maintaining the status quo.

Training: What are the tasks that someone needs to come prepared to perform without the time to learn on the job or time to look up the answers? After answering this question, you can narrow down the audience and learning objectives for either online training or classroom training. This will be true for any *delta* training, which is for the current audience that knows the job but needs to know how to work with the new change program, as well as ongoing training, which is for people joining the team after the change program roll-out. Within storying thinking, training is considered to be learning that is related to the half-pipe where the focus in on *how* and not *why*. In general, we usually rely too much on *training* to adopt and maintain the new status quo. There are usually better options upstream, or problem-solving is part of the job so *educating* (full-cycle learning) is required.

Educating: At the bottom of the Proficiency Waterfall, we find educating, because whatever was not stopped higher on the waterfall means that we are hoping that it will be caught by an educated person. This is true for operational and maintenance tasks. The organizational view of the story thinking cycle requires that the Automation phase be primarily routine and reactive, but here we still need individuals that have full-cycle learning to be able to solve for problems and fully participate as a stakeholder on related change projects.

It may seem counterintuitive that within the process of *change* that we have a step that requires us to *maintain*. But this is needed to reduce "change fatigue" and increase proficiency and productivity. Sometimes, we never make it this far in the cycle. I've seen cases where an organization prioritized a project to look into a new technology, and while they designed, developed, and tested a solution that would reduce time and errors in production, it never crossed that last line in the story thinking cycle from Affirmation to Automation. It never became the new routine. It was an idea that did not consider the requirements of *routine* within the *design* for that organization and culture.

In other cases, an organization "crosses the line" and initially adopts a new way of working. But before it can reach expected productivity measurements, the old "muscle memory" of the organization does not allow the change to stick. In general, change professionals over-rely on *training* as the solution to change. There are usually better options upstream in the proficiency waterfall. And sometimes, more education is needed, which goes beyond step-by-step training and provides the needed *understanding* for problem solving, *appreciation* for the steps that happen before your job role gets involved, and *consideration* for the steps that follow your job role. This is in addition to having an *empathy* for the customer's experience and journey in working with your organization. So, the Proficiency Waterfall is not just about removing people and working upstream, but about finding the right balance between all of the levels within the waterfall.

Multi-Generational Change

A change leader may attempt too much change within one cycle or generation by thinking that others can absorb as much as they can see, resulting in "change fatigue," project failures, or stakeholder rejection. So, some ambitious visions require multiple revolutions of change. Some changes could be viewed as objectionable and rejected if attempted all at once, so the intended change is broken into smaller cycles of change to cause "creeping normality" where the change is absorbed in smaller increments. Of course, this should only be done for ethical reasons. For example, someone may wake up in the hospital after a car accident to find out that their legs need to be amputated, the rest of their family in the car have all died, and the police think they are at fault—but you don't have to tell them this all at once because the amount of change may be too great to absorb.

Sometimes multi-generational change is the only way to incrementally build capabilities into your products. Instead of getting stopped within the Expectation phase, building towards a large goal, we can attempt "proximal" goals that produce "quick wins," but also confidence and material resources to continue (see figure 3.6).

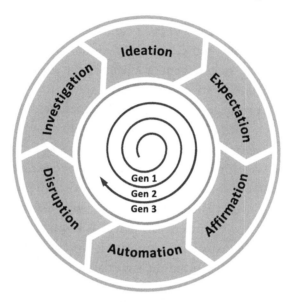

Figure 3.6—Multi-Generational Change

By understanding how to combine "R&D" with "Operations" (the full-cycle with the half-pipe), successful change leaders create a multi-generational change strategy so that each generation of an idea can be operationalized into a product or service, which can fund the next generation. For example, at Apple, Steve Jobs had a "multi-gen" strategy to sell the iPod (Gen 1), then the iPod with apps (Gen 2), then the iPhone (Gen 3), and then the iPad (Gen 4). Each new technology built on top of the previous technologies. With *technology*, each generation funds the R&D for the next generation. And with *people*, each generation "funds" the self-efficacy that people will need to have the *confidence* to attempt more and more complex challenges. Having a multi-generational change strategy, in some cases, is the only way to create "continuous" improvement.

Finally, sometimes the best way to affect change is not with a "multi-gen" *project* but with a "multi-gen" *culture*. Instead of change professionals just providing consulting for how to move from the current steady state to a future steady state, the better solution is to help organizations become agile, sustainable, learning environments. The rate of required change has increased within organizations. Supporting the "acceleration of change" goes beyond the "speed of change," as is also true with mathematics: acceleration is about the "change within the change." Now the change professional is needed to help us reach a new future state—one that is dynamic and changing—with an ever-changing pace of change. But this will require a deeper understanding of how *learning* itself is affected by story thinking—enjoy Part II: Learning.

Your Turn

Picture the story thinking cycle with the matching ILEDEM change model as you work through the tasks below:

- Create a personal mission and vision statement.
- What are you going to do differently and routinely now that the mission statement is defined for who you are, so that the vision can be pulled into reality?
- Identify a routine that could be improved and use the steps in the ILEDEM model.
- Design a "multi-gen" change strategy for your next project.
- For any given product that you are aware of, use the CLICK model to describe its components, links, implementation, composite, and knack; then make one or more changes and describe a new knack.
- List the ideas, people, processes, and technologies that are required to maintain your current state of Automation, and then describe the maintenance strategy to maintain principles, relationships, skills, and capabilities.

.

II

PART II: LEARNING

4

Continuous Feedback

"Unbelief in one thing springs from blind belief in another." — Georg Christoph Lichtenberg

Q: How can we create feedback loops within story thinking to support continuous improvement?

Learning Revolutions

In his 1962 classic book, *The Structure of Scientific Revolutions*, Thomas Kuhn challenged the scientific community with a new description for how learning occurs. Scientists like to believe that they are standing on solid ground—the sure footing of certainty—at all times. And from this mental place of certainty they believe that they are continually adding to their body of knowledge without ever needing to "go back to the drawing board" and start all over. But Kuhn only needed to point out what happened to the laws of motion, as described by Isaac Newton, after Albert Einstein arrived. Kuhn was describing the pattern of *scientific* revolutions, but more generically, he was describing *learning* revolutions.

Continuous learning involves continuous feedback, which can periodically show new observations that are outside the expected norm. In Einstein's case, the orbit of the planet Mercury was not following the model as predicted by Newton. But since Newton's model of planetary motion had stood for hundreds of years, the scientific community was not quick to jump to Einstein's new way of thinking.

Kuhn pointed out that revolutionary and transformational learning includes periods of confusion, where we try to maintain the current model for as long as possible—even in the face of evidence that we are in a state of unsustainable disruption—given the current model will not continue to work. This creates a breaking point that requires us to restart the cycle—to look beyond our current understanding and begin again (see figure 4.1).

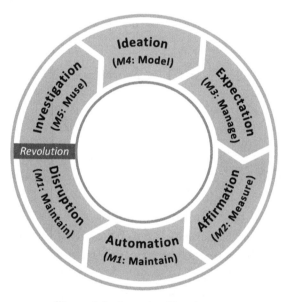

Figure 4.1—Learning Revolutions

In addition to scientific models, there are also economic models, business models, education models, and the list goes on, for every domain of study. Models attempt to describe nature in a way that allows us to make predictions about the future. For an example of a model within the medical domain, we once thought that stress was the key factor in getting ulcers and that surgery was the recommended treatment. But Dr. Barry Marshall questioned this paradigm and believed that in most cases an ulcer is produced by a bacterium, and patients could be easily cured with antibiotics. Of course, he was called a "quack" for many years, just like other pioneers—but his vindication came when he won the Nobel Prize in medicine. There is no domain of study that is exempt from learning revolutions. Klaus Schwab says in his book, *The Fourth Industrial Revolution*, "leaders must prove capable of changing their mental and conceptual frameworks and their organizing principles."

In the case of business models, instead of seeing revolutionary changes every few hundred years, the nature of consumer expectation requires that we reinvestigate and innovate new models on an annual basis. Given that a *model* is also referred to as the underlying *paradigm* from which we operate, Kuhn coined a term for the event within learning revolutions when a new model becomes accepted: the "paradigm shift." In his 1993 book, *Paradigms: The Business of Discovering the Future*, Joel Barker wonderfully introduced businesses to the academic world of mental models and paradigm shifts. But his book was positioned through the lens of *future studies*. Now it is time to approach the topic of paradigm shifts through the lens of *business as usual*. This will require a greater understanding of *learning* itself, and the various ways that feedback contributes to learning within our organizations. While we may count many events as "learning" events within a given organization, most of these activities are focused on individual "half-pipe" training and few are based on "full-cycle" transformational revolutions.

Quad-Loop Learning

The idea of "feedback loops" is built into the way we learn. Based on the difference between targeted goals and errors detected, these gaps provide feedback towards continuous improvement. Within the story thinking cycle, it is the Affirmation phase that plays this role to measure and provide four types of feedback (see figure 4.2): *Perceptive* feedback helps the Investigation phase when it is time to *muse* beyond our current understanding, requiring curiosity and exploration. *Inventive* feedback helps the Ideation phase when it is time to update our *model* or paradigm, requiring creativity to question our governing assumptions. *Productive* feedback helps the Expectation phase when it is time to update how we *manage* our efforts, requiring new strategies and commitments. The fourth type of feedback within quad-loop learning is *Compliant* feedback, which helps the Automation phase *maintain* efficiency, requiring programming or training to produce the desired codified or behavioral responses.

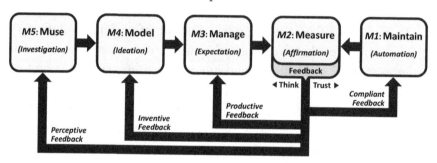

Figure 4.2—Quad-Loop Learning Framework

Where is Disruption? Within the framework of quad-loop learning, the Disruption phase is not visually represented. This is not due to its insignificance in story thinking, but actually due to its significance. It is not that it is missing, but that it is constant and inherent to continuous improvement. It is inherent to the nature of a learning organization, and fundamental for change leaders that don't wait for disruptions but instead acknowledge that the status quo may be a temporary condition.

Either disruptions are tolerated (Does Work), given current workarounds and system tolerances, or disruptions cannot be tolerated (Won't Work). In other words, either disruptions are accepted as part of the status quo ("stuff happens"), and therefore considered part of the reactive nature of Automation, or they are disruptions that we are not willing to live with, and therefore *produce* the four feedback loops for change. In their book, *Organizational Survival in the New World: The Intelligent Complex Adaptive System*, authors Alex and David Bennet tell us that organizations have dynamic balancing forces that drive organizational intelligence. These forces can be represented by the four feedback loops, which continuously affect modern knowledge-based organizations as they operate as intelligent complex adaptive systems.

For a simple example of using quad-loop learning, imagine that your daily job is to go into a forest and cut down the trees using an axe. You have been trained on how to swing an axe and how to sharpen an axe. Now imagine the thoughts you may have as you reflect upon your work:

- Compliant feedback says it may be time to stop for the day.
- Productive feedback says it may be time to sharpen the axe.
- Inventive feedback says it may be time to invent a chain saw.
- Perceptive feedback says it may be time to research another form of energy beyond wood.

Compliant feedback (for the Automation phase) supports learning related to our reactive memorization and repetitive behaviors for following current rules and operating norms. We focus on this type of feedback when we *trust* that the answer is already known, and we want to have the information or behaviors repeated to match expectations without exception and without "reinventing the wheel." Success measures include: compliance with expected operational and maintenance activities, predictable efficiency and effectiveness, a balance of human and artificial automation, and routines that align with core values.

Productive feedback (for the Expectation phase) supports learning related to our reflective actions, which could be driven by a known strategy or simple trial and error. We focus on this type of feedback when we think that reaching a goal has been narrowed to finding the right technique. Success measures include: clear expectations and goals, measurable progress, development of strategies, procedures, and people, and delivering on commitments.

Inventive feedback (for the Ideation phase) supports learning related to the model or underlying paradigm that drives our current methods. We focus on this type of feedback when we think that a solution will require more than a different technique within the current design or theory and will require a new way of thinking for how to approach a solution. Success measures include: creative solutions beyond half-pipe thinking, brainstorming and diversity of initial ideas (opening), transparency in the selection process (closing), articulating error preferences and tradeoff decisions, articulating risks and rewards, and aligning designs and plans with the strategic vision.

Perceptive feedback (for the Investigation phase) supports learning related to discernment and awareness of the larger situation, deeper analysis, or higher truth. We focus on this type of feedback when we think that more basic research is needed before looking at inventive, productive, or compliant feedback. Success measures include: first-principle discoveries beyond half-pipe analogies, finding root causes and root factors, impartial and objective questioning, and applying systems thinking, reframing, and unlearning.

Goal feedback (for the Affirmation phase) is not associated with one specific loop, but rather built into this intelligent complex adaptive system. We focus on this type of feedback when we think that the current goal is too easy or too difficult to obtain regardless of efforts through the four feedback loops. This level of goal setting is associated with strategic planning more than the underlying continuous improvement cycles as we saw in the last chapter. Success measures include: strategic recognition of problems and opportunities, prioritizing feedback, and setting obtainable goals.

Readers familiar with the term "Double-Loop Learning" will recognize the "single-loop" as M2 to M3, providing productive feedback for how we manage, and the "double-loop" as M2 to M4 providing inventive feedback for why the underlying model may need to change. The primary reasons that this framework is replaced by quad-loop learning are: 1) Descriptions of "single-loop" learning conflate examples that are procedurally explicit (M3) and codified (M1). 2) There is too much focus on the loops without accurate names for the loops or descriptions for the nodes. 3) It is an incomplete framework when compared to quad-loop learning for identifying feedback types.

Readers familiar with the term "Triple-Loop Learning," which is just "double-loop" learning with an extra loop tacked on to reflect on our learning, may wonder why quad-loop learning does not have a feedback loop for a meta-analysis of the learning process. The reason is because by definition, "meta" refers to a level above (super) or below (sub) and should not exist at the same level as the primary flow. To understand "meta" as a sub to the main flow of quad-loop learning, refer to "conceptional" knowledge in the next chapter which is a sub-topic for metacognitive knowledge within each phase. To understand "meta" as a super-topic, imagine a stack of pancakes with each level representing a story thinking cycle operating above the one below, with "stories all the way down" as our meta learning representation.

Ignite Your Muse

Ignite your Muse! That's right—not your *fuse* (M1), but your *muse* (M5). To *muse* simply means "to think about something carefully and thoroughly." We acknowledge that we are learners seeking continuous improvement, but we need to consider the types of feedback that occupy most of our time. We may be so busy learning how to be *compliant*, and how to be more *productive*, that we forget our larger journey and the revolutionary learning only found when we learn how to be more *perceptive*. Review the Quad-Loop Learning Summary Table below (see table 4.1) and fill-in the row that asks for the percentage of your time that you spend in each phase. You can do this for yourself and also for your organization.

	Muse (M5)	Model (M4)	Manage (M3)	Measure (M2)	Maintain (M1)
Story Phases	Investigation	Ideation	Expectation	Affirmation	Automation
Feedback Loops	Perceptive	Inventive	Productive	Goal Setting	Compliant
Underlying Question	Wherefore	Why	How	What	Isn't It So
Thought Control	—	—	—	Authority	Programming
Percentage of My Time:					

Table 4.1—Quad-Loop Learning Summary

From the table above, we see that the underlying question that drives our thinking about the Model (M4) is "why." And the underlying question that drives our thinking within Muse (M5) is "wherefore." While most of us today are familiar with the term "why," most of us are not familiar with the term "wherefore."

"Wherefore art thou, Romeo?" This was the question that defined the plot in William Shakespeare's classic story of Romeo and Juliet. In Shakespeare's time, the term "wherefore" was understood to be a question related to "why," not a question related to "where." So, "Wherefore art thou, Romeo" is not Juliet asking for where Romeo is, but for the "why of why" that he must "exist." Over time, we have dropped the use of the term "wherefore," seeing it as simply redundant with the term "why." To understand a topic, people once asked for "the whys and wherefores" of that topic. Still today, an Internet search for "whys and wherefores" will produce results for various topics because some writers still use this phrase to describe *all* of the underlying reasons.

In his book, *Start with Why*, Simon Sinek describes how great leaders inspire everyone to take action. Instead of starting our communications with *what* we do or *how* we do it, it is much more powerful to start our communications with our beliefs and passion for *why* we do what we do. In his equally compelling book, *Find Your Why*, Simon Sinek provides a guide for *discovering* your purpose. We can think of this as the "why of why" or "wherefore" from which we emerge with our "why." This is an important step, sometimes missed, by those who speak passionately about what they believe in, yet it is clear they have not actually done their homework or adequately researched the topic. So, another way that I describe "finding your why" is to "start with wherefore."

In our attempt to understand the wholeness of a topic, we are usually led to the idea of "systems thinking." This extension of cause-and-effect thinking shows us that effects provide a feedback loop into the next cause, helping us to understand that what we call an "effect" is actually *part* of the next "cause." We move from *systems* thinking to *symbiotic* thinking when we realize that the very concept of "cause" cannot *exist* without the concept of "effect." The deeper relationship is not from causality, but from balanced existence. Would the concept of "day" even need to exist if not also for the concept of "night?" Would we have a need for the term "summer" if not also for the term "winter?" In the physical universe, we find that since there is such a thing as "matter" that there is also "antimatter."

In their series of books on *The Profundity and Bifurcation of Change*, Bennet, et al. summarize: *"Symmetry* is proportional or balanced harmony, and tightly linked with the concept of beauty. The very existence of a thing or idea *requires* the existence of something else. As we develop our symbiotic thinking, we see that "supply and demand" is not just a single business concept, but two concepts that exist because the other also exists. We now view the old and new testaments of the Bible, not as a contradiction but as a completion, since grace (new) cannot exist without law (old). And we begin to understand the nature of quantum physics where two states must potentially exist at the same time; for example, consider the famous thought experiment of Schrodinger's cat which is both alive and dead. Things that don't make sense using systems thinking begin to make sense using symbiotic thinking."

Learning to *muse* means more than just using analytical thinking, statistics, and root cause analysis—it also means using symbiotic thinking. Does lightning just travel downward? With symbiotic thinking we would understand that if there is a *reaching down* then there is also a *reaching up*, and indeed modern photography has captured the phenomenon of *upward streamers*. If there is a counterfeit then there must also be an authentic, and vice versa. Can the concept of *public* continue to exist without the protection of *privacy* laws? Exercising our symbiotic thinking is the beginning of discernment, inference, and speculation, which drives our explorations within M5.

Sometimes, as we are researching to solve a problem, we may realize that there are two sides to the problem. And sometimes, in determining a root cause we may realize that the problem is us. I heard a joke about an old man that wanted to test his wife's hearing. He sat her on the couch, then walked to the other side of the room and said, "Can you hear me?" He heard no response from her so he got closer to her and asked, "Can you hear me?" Again, he heard no response so he walked all the way back to her and asked, "Can you hear me?" She said: "For the *third* time, I said *yes* I can hear you."

Perception and perspective are intricately linked. One exists because of the other—each having the seeds of the other, as represented in the yin-yang symbol—the balance between two opposites. I am hearing what I hear because of the external sounds but also because of my own hearing condition. I am seeing what I am seeing because of the view outside my window but also because I am *not* looking at what is in the room behind me. I am looking for a light switch to solve for the room being so dark because I have not realized that I am still wearing my sunglasses. If you have worked as a consultant or leadership coach long enough, eventually you will have to tell the CEO that hired you that *he/she* is the root cause of the issues facing the organization.

When reaching the "why of why" (in M5) and realizing that *we* are part of the *answer* to what we find, there is an opportunity for transformational change, and also the possibility of retreating back to maintain (in M1) our current thinking. None of us enjoy looking into the mirror to discover our part of the problem we face for which we own. We seem somehow naturally oblivious to the idea that we are not the good and fixed reference from which all things are measured (in M2). Discovering and acknowledging this concept (in M5) requires more than learning *about*, it requires learning *within*—that envisions a new model for ourselves (in M4), with a new way to think about how we cooperate (in M3) towards a new set of goals and standards for ourselves (in M2) that will lead to a new routine in how we operate (in M1). This is when we realize that we were born as learners—a special type of learner; we were born as an intelligent complex adaptive system. This is the same level of understanding required of generalized artificial intelligence if it is to become fully self-aware.

Your Turn

Picture the Quad-Loop Learning Framework as you work through the tasks below:

- RPM is defined as the speed of rotation, and for machines it means "revolutions per minute," but for organizations, we could see it as "revolutions per month." To help recognize the difference between transformational changes based on *full* revolutions versus compliant training, keep a monthly count of learning events based on full revolutions of change.
- For the improvement projects you participated in over the last year, what percentage relates to each of the four feedback loops?
  - _____ % of projects were based on Compliant Feedback.
  - _____ % of projects were based on Productive Feedback.
  - _____ % of projects were based on Inventive Feedback.
  - _____ % of projects were based on Perceptive Feedback.
- For each of the example words in the table below (see table 4.2), look up each term, using several different sources, and see how they align with your current understanding. For example, look up the definition for "Gestalt" and consider how you currently acquire meaningful perceptions. For another example, look up the definition for "Discernment," especially if you could not understand why there are two rows for words that start with the letter: "D."

Example Words	Muse (M5)	Model (M4)	Manage (M3)	Measure (M2)	Maintain (M1)
Starts with: A	Awakening	Assumptions	Action	Achievement	Association
Starts with: B	Beyond	Belief System	Begin	Become	Behavioral
Starts with: C	Curiosity	Creativity	Commitment	Consequence	Codified
Starts with: D	Discernment	Design	Dedicated	Decisive	Disciplined
Starts with: D	Deception	Delusion	Duplicity	Defensive	Distracted
Starts with: E	Explore	Exemplar	Effort	Evaluate	Emotional
Starts with: F	Find	Framework	Faith	Feedback	Fact
Starts with: G	Gestalt	Governing	Guideline	Goal	Gifted

Table 4.2—Quad-Loop Learning Example Words

5

Objective-based Learning

"If history repeats itself, and the unexpected always happens, how incapable must Man be of learning from experience." — George Bernard Shaw

Q: Why did I love learning yet hate school?

The Objective of Education

What is the objective of education? Dr. Martin Luther King Jr. once said that "the function of education is to teach one to think intensively and to think critically. But education which stops with efficiency may prove the greatest menace to society" (speech at Morehouse College, 1948). Within story thinking, we can describe this philosophy as providing a "Full-Cycle Education," focusing on intellectual *curiosity* over intellectual *conviction* (see figure 5.1). But B. F. Skinner had a different point of view, writing that "education is the establishing of behavior" (Skinner, 1953). We can describe this philosophy as providing a "Half-Pipe Education," focusing on intellectual *conviction* over intellectual *curiosity*.

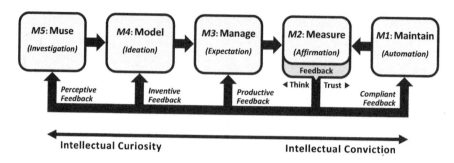

Figure 5.1—Intellectual Curiosity vs. Intellectual Conviction

Education is a topic that we all should be interested in improving. Some readers of this book work in childhood education, or higher-education, or within a corporate training and development department. But other readers are still affected by education, directly as a student, and indirectly as a consumer and citizen. Most readers may be familiar with the recent educational focus on STEM topics (Science, Technology, Engineering, and Mathematics). And some readers may be familiar with the educational focus on using computers and other technologies to teach these topics. Yet most people are completely unfamiliar with the more important aspect of education, known as the "pedagogy," which is the underlying philosophy and strategies that drive the educational system. In the fourth industrial revolution, "leaders need to prepare workforces and develop education models to work with, and alongside, increasingly capable, connected and intelligent machines" (Schwab, 2017).

The "Progress" in American Education

In 1956, Benjamin Bloom published his work on how he and his team had organized and classified classroom learning objectives. In the introduction to his *Taxonomy of Educational Objectives, Handbook 1*, he acknowledges that the idea for a taxonomy of learning objectives was formed by college examiners (not teachers), and that there was concern the taxonomy "might lead to *fragmentation* and atomization of educational purposes such that the parts and pieces finally placed into the classification might be very different from the more complete objective with which one started."

Without an underlying framework, like the structure of the story, the "fragmentation" to a student's learning was inevitable. The focus was on *testing* fragments of a lesson rather than *understanding* the holistic lesson—just to help the testers create "banks" of test items "to reduce their labor in preparing annual comprehensive exams" (Krathwohl, 2002). Below is the taxonomy published in 1956 by Bloom and his team, with six categories of cognitive objectives (see table 5.1).

Higher-Level Objectives			Lower-Level Objectives		
Evaluation	Synthesis	Analysis	Application	Comprehension	Knowledge

Table 5.1—Bloom's Taxonomy First Edition (1956)

Notice the six types of objectives created by Bloom and his team of testers, with "evaluation" listed as the highest order of thinking, and "knowledge" as the lowest level. While most agreed that there were learning objectives related to simply remembering knowledge at the lower end of the taxonomy, it was not apparent that the "higher level" objectives were organized in a meaningful way.

A "stakeholder" is someone who has an interest or some "stake" in a given topic, so the stakeholders related to education include the parents, taxpayers, students, teachers, employers, and also the testers. But for some reason, since 1956, the education community has allowed the testers to have more weight in the decisions than the other stakeholders. If other stakeholders say they need to teach something, but the testers say they don't know how to test for it, then it is not taught. This is called the "tail wagging the dog" within education. It is also called the "tyranny of the testers."

It is important to understand that America already had a good education system before the fundamental approach to learning was changed by the widespread adoption of the frameworks put forward by B.F. Skinner and Benjamin Bloom. B.F. Skinner studied how to condition rats and pigeons by focusing on behavioral outcomes of learning (Skinner, 1953), and his approaches were later adopted by American educators. By 1971 (Sept 20), he was featured on the cover of *Time Magazine*, accompanied by his rats and pigeons, with the article titled "*Skinner's Utopia: Panacea, or Path to Hell?*" in reference to his latest book, *Beyond Freedom and Dignity* (1971).

In 1983, separate from the work done by Bloom and his team, David Merrill (Merrill, 1983) published his Component Display Theory (CDT), that included a "Performance" dimension and also a "Content" dimension, which together produced his Performance-Content Classification Matrix (see table 5.2).

	Find	Use	Remember
Principle			
Procedure			
Concept			
Fact			

Table 5.2—Merrill's Performance-Content Classification Matrix (1983)

At the lower-level of educational objectives, he used the term "Remember" instead of Bloom's term "Knowledge" and at the higher level he used the term "Find." He described this dimension of the matrix as a level of "Performance" such that "Find" is the performance that requires the student to derive or invent a new abstraction; "Use" is the performance that requires the student to apply some abstraction to a specific case; and "Remember" is the performance that requires the student to search their memory in order to recognize or reproduce previously stored information. Notice that this follows the *process* of learning instead of mere *categories* of exam objectives used by Bloom (contributing to fragmentation).

Merrill also recognized, with the Content dimension, that for each of the performance requirements, there could be a different type of knowledge content involved, which are: Fact, Concept, Procedure, and Principle. For example, a learning objective that expects students to remember a Fact might be taught using flash cards, but a learning objective that expects students to remember a Procedure might require demonstrations and practice. This approach provided instructional designers with a more-refined method towards writing learning objectives and creating learning experiences.

During this same timeframe, in 1983, the critical report, *A Nation at Risk*, along with other similar reports, showed that American education was failing the students and the nation due to a deficiency in higher-level thinking and reasoning skills. Given that Bloom's Taxonomy was more widely used by teachers than Merrill's work, a recommendation was made to update it to address these concerns.

In 2001, Bloom's Taxonomy was revised such that the original terms were changed and rearranged, and a new dimension was added for different types of knowledge—creating a matrix (see table 5.3). Notice how much the revised version of Bloom's Taxonomy borrows from Merrill's design.

	Create	Evaluate	Analyze	Apply	Understand	Remember
Metacognitive						
Procedural						
Conceptual						
Factual						

Table 5.3—Bloom's Taxonomy Revised Edition (2001)

Within the matrix of Bloom's Revised Taxonomy, the highest-level objective has been changed from "Evaluation" to "Create." In keeping with the idea that there must only be six categories, we notice that this addition was done at the expense of removing "Synthesis," which is different from "Create," and still a needed type of learning objective.

Bloom's Revised Taxonomy adopts a matrix idea identical to Merrill, and the process dimension is called the "cognitive" process dimension, in keeping with the original idea of separating "cognitive" objectives from "affective" objectives and "psychomotor" objectives.

Sadly, this adherence to a 1956 idea continues to perpetuate the problem of fragmentation by removing "values" from the lesson-based learning process, to isolate them within Bloom's "affective" domain for *emotion*-based ideas. Values formed through the "lessons learned" process found in the story thinking pattern are not simply "emotion-based" ideas. Within a business, it would be seen as preposterous to suggest that the organization's values are merely "emotion-based," not "cognitive-based," and should not be integrated into the thinking and learning programs of the organization. Yet this is what was done for the organization called *America*.

The organizational learning objective called "appreciate" was essentially removed from the classroom, by placing it in the "affective domain" list of objectives instead of the "cognitive domain." Purportedly this was done because the testers say they don't know how to measure or test for it. Given that Bloom's "affective domain" objectives are not routinely taught or tested as part of official tests within Education, the net result, whether intended or not, is that America's foundational values for intellectual freedom have been effectively removed from the educational process. Now, some are left wondering if this fragmentation was just a *side-effect* of Bloom's project, or the *purpose*. Some interesting books for the curious include *Deliberate Dumbing Down of America* by Charlotte Iserbyt, and *Crimes of the Educators* by Samuel Blumenfeld and Alex Newman, which purport to provide evidence of *intentional* educational decline in America.

The fundamental problem with Bloom's approach within the "cognitive domain," which creates cognitive fragmentation, is that it is a model based on a presumed hierarchy of exam complexity, instead of using a model based on the process of learning. Watching children create and test their ideas for just a few minutes should indicate that these are not "higher-order skills" which students should only attempt in higher level courses, as Bloom's Taxonomy has been implemented by many teachers. They are skills that are harder for the testers to evaluate—but are simply the beginning of the story thinking cycle. This is where people have the intellectual freedom to question within full-cycle learning instead of just memorizing provided answers from a half-pipe education.

The combined effect by the work of B.F. Skinner and Benjamin Bloom on the American education system could possibly be justified in Industrial Age (first and second industrial revolutions) settings, where most workers would be trained to perform repetitive, manual labor. But in the Fourth Industrial Revolution, our workforce cannot be prepared with such an educational approach. Even with the 2001 revision of Bloom's Taxonomy, the fragmented design continues to influence educational outcomes which have not significantly improved, and it was time to rethink the pedagogy framework that drives education in America.

The Lewis Learning Objective Framework

Instead of fragmented categories of exam objectives driving the overall educational process, Lewis' learning-knowledge matrix (see table 5.4) was created to operate from story thinking and the process of learning. Expanding on Merrill's approach, the primary dimension of the Learning-Knowledge Matrix is based on the sequence of learning, not categories for testing. This Learning-Knowledge Matrix is not just another *rearrangement* of objective categories, but a *realignment* with the story thinking pattern.

	Story Thinking: Full-Cycle Learning				Half-Pipe Learning
	Muse (M5)	Model (M4)	Manage (M3)	Measure (M2)	Maintain (M1)
Collaborative (C5)					
Conceptional (C4)					
Consequential (C3)					
Contextual (C2)					
Concise (C1)					

Table 5.4—Lewis Learning-Knowledge Matrix

The Knowledge dimension of the Learning-Knowledge Matrix expands on the work by Merrill and Bloom. For each of the phases within the framework of quad-loop learning, there are five key types of knowledge that should be considered during objective-based learning: concise, contextual, consequential, conceptional, and collaborative, as detailed below:

Concise Knowledge: Why did *Factual* change to *Concise* Knowledge? A *fact* is what we accept as true and trusted for now. Calling something a *fact* does not mean it is true, otherwise we would not also need the term "fact-checking." Also, a fact is something that we can attempt to prove to be true, which does not help us understand the specific knowledge required to move around the entire story thinking cycle. For example, understanding how the scientific method has been applied through story thinking requires recognizing a concise non-example observation (in Disruption), that drove a concise question (in Investigation), which led to the formulation of a concise hypothesis (in Ideation), which required a concise experiment (in Expectation), concluding with a concise test (in Affirmation), which if true we would share the study so others could reference the source and call it a "fact." To work at the higher levels of learning, we need to learn how to be concise, with our hypothesis, experiment, and test. And when maintaining concise knowledge, we need to remember that what we accepted as a fact yesterday may not be true today. It becomes more difficult to move from "trust" back to "think" when we cannot separate the difference between concise knowledge and factual knowledge.

Contextual Knowledge: Why did *Conceptual* change to *Contextual* Knowledge? In addition to generic or abstract concepts, we also need to ensure that we can see the concept within concise examples, and understand that any given concept related to concise knowledge is just one of many, given the relativity of context. This is related to the topic of taxonomy vs ontology, where a taxonomy shows one declared way that individual items connect in a hierarchy, but an ontology allows for several hierarchical views based on the context. This term forces us to not only connect examples to a concept but to also consider additional concepts given the context.

Consequential Knowledge: Why did *Procedural* change to *Consequential* Knowledge? This type of knowledge is temporal, instead of contextual, meaning that it is related to time. We recognize that a *procedure* provides the *prescriptive* steps that an *individual* needs to take in order to perform a desired outcome, whereas a *process* provides the *descriptive* steps an *organization* needs to take, usually encapsulating several procedures, to perform a desired outcome. Whereas Bloom and Merrill focus attention on the procedure, we recognize that knowledge of the broader process that we work within is also required in the modern workplace.

Conceptional Knowledge: Why did *Metacognitive* change to *Conceptional* Knowledge? These ideas relate to the conception of the idea, so some call this the metacognitive *level*, or deeper level of knowledge. Metacognition relates to the cognition about cognition. But the idea of "meta" goes beyond the "knowing about knowing" — it also includes the thinking about learning, the learning about thinking, the learning about learning, the thinking about thinking, the feelings of knowing, and the knowing of feelings. Conceptional knowledge is related to how an idea is conceived and formed. This difference allows us to expand our thinking to include, for example, that the meta source may be an emotion and not cognitive. Or it may be related to self-concept which is different than thinking about subject-concepts. And it allows us to expand our thinking in terms of levels. Instead of thinking of only one level of knowing underneath what we know, there can be many. Instead of just describing a pattern for solving problems, conceptional knowledge also describes the unlearning and relearning of these patterns. It is not enough to focus on how I search, frame, define, construct, evaluate, think, and learn—we need to also build into our learning expectations the ability to research, reframe, redefine, reconstruct, reevaluate, rethink, and unlearn. The process of mental construction is not simply "one and done." It is understanding the genesis and process of mental *reconstruction* that is key to continuous learning.

Collaborative Knowledge: Why has *Collaborative* Knowledge been added? This is based on the idea that learning is also a social experience. In addition to knowing how to research, design, and develop, workers today also need to know how to co-research, codesign, and codevelop. In addition to knowing how to estimate and judge, workers today also need to know how to critique and resolve. When working together in a learning organization, understanding the framework of story thinking along with expected collaborative activities along the way, provides for shared understanding and faster revolutions for the team around the story thinking cycle.

You may have noticed that when you take a course, at school or at work, they will tell you at the beginning of the course what you should be able to *do* after taking the class. A common approach may look like this: "Upon taking this course, you will be able to DESCRIBE the concept of X, LIST the items of Y, and RECITE the definition of Z." These lists of "learning objectives" are valuable for setting course expectations for the student and the teacher.

Teachers that believe education is primarily about establishing behavior adhere to the philosophy of "radical behaviorism" and expect all learning verbs to be directly measurable through an individual's behavior. These teachers may initially be frustrated with the story thinking approach towards learning objectives since all the verbs may not be directly observable when testing behaviors and will require creative evaluation techniques. Teachers that believe that education cannot be provided or guided and must be constructed entirely by each learner adhere to the philosophy of "radical constructivism" and may reject the idea of learning objective verbs entirely.

The story thinking approach towards learning objectives strikes a *balance* between radical behaviorism and radical constructivism to provide a guided tour through the natural story thinking pattern of learning. Below are example learning objective verbs (see table 5.5) for each phase of the learning dimension (M1-M5), with specific examples from the knowledge dimension (C1-C5) identified as well.

| | Story Thinking: Full-Cycle Learning | | | | | | Half-Pipe Learning | | | |
| | Muse (M5) | | Model (M4) | | Manage (M3) | | Measure (M2) | | Maintain (M1) | |
	Explore	Analyze	Synthesize	Envision	Create	Apply	Evaluate	Understand	Remember	Practice
	anticipate[4]	ascertain[3]	categorize[1]	axiomatize[4]	adapt[2]	act[3]	achieve[3]	analogize[4]	associate[2]	avert[3]
	benchmark[2]	audit[3]	classify[2]	codesign[5]	attempt[3]	assemble[3]	balance[4]	appreciate[4]	document[5]	comply[5]
	collect[3]	codetermine[5]	combine[2]	define[2]	build[3]	complete[1]	calculate[3]	cite[1]	identify[1]	coordinate[5]
	co-research[5]	contrast[2]	compare[2]	design[1]	change[3]	compute[3]	choose[3]	debate[5]	list[2]	gamify[4]
	discern[4]	deconstruct[3]	correlate[2]	forecast[3]	codevelop[5]	configure[2]	confirm[1]	deduce[4]	locate[2]	operate[3]
	discover[2]	determine[4]	corroborate[5]	formulate[4]	construct[1]	cooperate[5]	critique[5]	describe[2]	match[1]	perform[3]
	elicit[5]	diagnose[4]	extrapolate[3]	hypothesize[4]	customize[2]	demonstrate[5]	estimate[2]	elaborate[3]	memorialize[1]	preserve[3]
	find[1]	differentiate[2]	frame[2]	plan[1]	develop[3]	exploit[2]	judge[2]	explain[3]	mnemonicize[4]	react[3]
	infer[4]	dissect[3]	organize[2]	postulate[5]	devise[4]	make[3]	motivate[5]	interpret[4]	personalize[4]	recognize[1]
	investigate[3]	dissociate[2]	patternize[4]	predict[4]	encourage[5]	proceduralize[4]	reevaluate[3]	justify[3]	recall[1]	rehearse[3]
	question[4]	distinguish[3]	rearrange[2]	prevent[3]	experiment[4]	reconstruct[3]	refute[1]	persuade[5]	recite[1]	reward[4]
	research[3]	examine[3]	reframe[2]	propose[5]	illustrate[1]	repair[3]	resolve[5]	prioritize[2]	reference[1]	schedule[3]
	sample[2]	factor[1]	simplify[1]	redefine[2]	optimize[2]	replicate[3]	set goals[4]	recommend[5]	reflect[4]	select[2]
	speculate[4]	inspect[3]	systematize[4]	repurpose[2]	prototype[3]	solve[4]	standardize[4]	reprioritize[2]	remind[5]	supervise[5]
	survey[5]	normalize[1]	unify[4]	theorize[4]	strategize[4]	use[3]	test[3]	summarize[2]	unlearn[4]	train[3]

1=Concise,   2=Contextual,   3=Consequential,   4=Conceptional,   5=Collaborative

Table 5.5—Lewis Learning-Knowledge Matrix Example Verbs

These learning objective verbs are useful for both gathering learning requirements as well as evaluating learning outcomes. In the Industrial Age (second industrial revolution), most workers would be trained to perform repetitive, manual labor. So, the learning designers would interview experts and perform a "task analysis" to capture the best techniques for each job. The questions they would ask were mainly around "how" the job is best performed, so the task analysis and the post-instruction tests used many of the same verbs, which are now listed under M1 in the table above. But in the Fourth Industrial Revolution, learning designers interview "*knowledge* workers" to perform a "*cognitive* task analysis" to capture the *thinking* behind their performance. The questions they need to ask a knowledge worker include the entire table from above. Then learning experiences are created from these verbs, and finally the test questions are also based on the same verbs. With Bloom's taxonomy, the learning objective verbs are too fragmented from the actual work and cannot be used to perform a cognitive task analysis—another indication of the need for its replacement.

As some educators have started to use this approach, they ask why the verb "define" is not listed under M1 since we see this in many Bloom Taxonomy verb tables under the category for "Remember." The answer is that to "define" requires that we "discover and set forth the meaning of" which is a mental activity under M4 where we envision a new way to see and describe something. When most teachers ask students to "define" a term, what they are really asking them to do is "recite" the definition that was provided. So, this is why we see "recite" and not "define" as a learning verb within M1.

As some educators have started to use this approach, they also ask where the verb "decide" is within the above table. This is a broad term, so the more specific variations of "decide" are used based on where we are within story thinking. For example, in M1 we see "identify, associate, and select." In M2 we see "choose, judge, and set goals." In M3 we see "strategize, optimize, and solve." In M4 we see "hypothesize, categorize, and theorize." And in M5 we see "infer, ascertain, and determine."

The classical learning objective related to "determine" comes from the field of electrical engineering where it arose as a problem given to students, known as the "Black Box" (Ashby, 1964). Given a sealed (usually black) box with input terminals and output meters, an engineering student would have to *determine* the function and components *inside* the box by connecting the input terminals to various voltages, etc., and observing the output. The concept of determining the contents and configuration of the "Black Box" through outside interactions has spread beyond the engineering lab and is a great example of a creative learning objective requiring higher-order thinking skills.

To decide through logic, we see "deduce," which requires *deductive* reasoning, within M2 as a specific type of understanding, but *inductive* reasoning requires starting from M5. When picturing this within the story thinking cycle, we see that induction happens in the full-cycle and deduction happens in the half-pipe. So, a half-pipe education only provides the illusion of reasoning skills, through deduction, unchecked by induction. One famous example of deduction-only logic is: "God is Love. Love is Blind. Ray Charles is Blind. Ray Charles is God." It reminds us that even when we think we are being logical, we may still be stuck in the half-pipe, using only what some now call "simulated thinking," with reasons only from deduction, analogy, and association.

Given that this approach recognizes that *values* are related to "lessons learned" from the story thinking cycle, some have asked how values have been integrated into our cognitive objective verbs (instead of Bloom's "affective domain" for "emotion-based" ideas). Values are found in the learning of lessons and are articulated through objectives within the category "Understand" with verbs like: appreciate, debate, explain, justify, and prioritize. While the teaching of *organizational* learning objectives requires that the next generation appreciates foundational values (otherwise, history repeats itself as we relearn hard-won lessons), the argument that some testers use to not test for the learning verb of "appreciate" is that it is an "emotion-based" idea. Other testers will say that they don't know how to test for this objective so it can't be taught. Ultimately, we may find that values are the key to educating the next generation, as they provide lessons learned from story thinking which are generational in the process of achievement—as well as collapse.

Like all domains, educators have a language that they use within their circle of professionals. Two terms which they use, related to learning objectives, are "formative evaluation" and "summative evaluation," and they ask how these terms fit within story thinking. A *formative* evaluation happens in M5 (Investigation phase of the cycle) to examine, ascertain, and determine the current gaps that may exist in the student's performance, so that a specific plan can be applied to help them reach required goals. This is usually achieved with targeted quizzes and homework assignments which do not contribute significantly to the student's overall grade. A *summative* evaluation happens in M2 (Affirmation phase of the cycle) to test, calculate, and judge the student's performance at the end of the course. This is usually achieved with a final cumulative test or final paper. Both types of evaluation are needed, so it is the balance in time and grade weight that is usually debated towards keeping score.

Learning Questions

W. Edwards Deming is quoted as saying, "Without questions, there is no learning." You may have noticed that every chapter in this book starts with a question. You may have also noticed that in the Learning-Knowledge Example Verbs matrix above (see table 5.5), that "question" is an expected activity when we begin to muse and explore (in the Investigation phase of the story thinking cycle). Given that all knowledge is an answer to a question, providing students with "learning questions" provides them with a better starting place to understand the answers they will have when they reach the M1 "learning objectives." Starting with a question will let students experience the thought process of Full-Cycle Learning and reach the Half-Pipe through understanding instead of just memorization.

Most people know that Albert Einstein created a theory of relativity. But most people do not know that this theory came from his ability to formulate this question: "What would I see if I could ride on a beam of light?" Imagine signing up for a physics class, and before seeing the learning objectives (e.g. "You will be able to describe the theory of relativity") that you see this learning question: "What would you see if you could ride on a beam of light?" Now I am curious to understand the answer, and also how we got from the question to the answer. While some teachers may feel that providing students with questioning skills will undermine the authority they need to deliver the answers in the classroom, other teachers interested in providing Full-Cycle Learning will include learning questions along with the learning objectives.

Some students have more intellectual curiosity than others. Through tests (Cacioppo, 1984) we can determine which students have a higher "need for cognition." Even without the teacher providing learning questions, their minds are constantly trying to connect the dots needed for Full-Cycle Learning while the rest of the class is engaged in Half-Pipe Learning. The teacher may note that they are "not a fast learner" and also do not perform as well on exams as other students. But these students align exactly with the research on mental model theory (Mayer, 1989). They seem to take longer to learn than other students because they are connecting the Half-Pipe Learning back into the necessary mental models to make sense of the memorized instruction, and they do not seem to recite basic names and facts as well as other students. If the teacher's exam included questions requiring problem-solving instead of just reciting, they would perform better on the tests than the other students. When we provide the learning questions for the *entire* class, and include learning objectives related to Full-Cycle Learning, we change the standard and definition for what it means to be a good student.

Your Turn

Picture the Learning-Knowledge Matrix Example Verbs (see table 5.5) and the Lewis Learning Objective Framework (see figure 5.2) as you work through the tasks below:

- For teachers and instructional designers that currently use Bloom's Taxonomy as the foundational categories of learning objectives, add three additional learning categories to your work (Explore, Envision, and Practice) to be able to align your lessons with the story thinking pattern of learning. (Note: *Synthesis* was already included in the original 1956 version of Bloom's Taxonomy).

- For teachers and instructional designers, ensure that learning objective verbs include several examples from the *Knowledge* dimension of the Learning-Knowledge Matrix (C1 through C5).
- For teachers and instructional designers, add a few key learning *questions* to each syllabus to accompany the list of learning *objectives*.

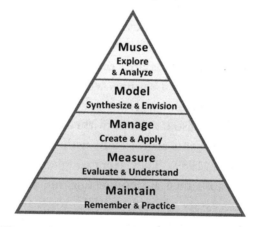

Figure 5.2—Lewis Learning Objective Framework

6

Continuous Learning

"The person who follows the crowd will usually go no further than the crowd. The person who walks alone is likely to find himself in places no one has ever seen before." — Albert Einstein

Q: How can organizations produce thought leaders?

Learning Time

The terms "continuous learning" and "continuous improvement" are now probably familiar terms, but just what type of learning is continually taking place? The quad-loop learning framework allows us to point to the specific phases of the story thinking cycle where we are responding to specific types of feedback. It also allows us to compare the amount of time that we spend on feedback related to becoming more inventive versus becoming more productive.

Are we trying to create something new or trying to get "work" done? Are we spending more time in M4 and M5 (Ideation and Investigation), or more time in M1, M2, and M3 (Automation, Affirmation, and Expectation)? Many organizations say that they spend time towards continuous learning and continuous improvement, but upon inspection we may find only improvements in productive outcomes, not inventive outcomes (see figure 6.1).

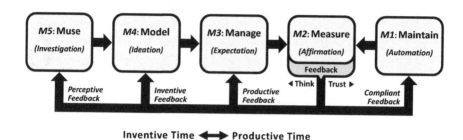

Figure 6.1—Inventive Learning Time vs. Productive Learning Time

The choice of Inventive Time versus Productive Time forces us to ask what the right *balance* should be for our organization and for each individual. If an organization is divided between the Research & Development department and the Operations department, then the organization may have a balance in inventive time versus productive time. But today, we usually find that organizations are structured such that the leaders and workers are required to create this balance for themselves.

Learning S-Curve

For each knowledge worker, as their inventive time increases, their productive time decreases, and vice versa. For example, as we are developing from a Novice to an Expert, we eventually begin to ask questions about the underlying assumptions and models that drive the way we have learned each topic. As we spend time thinking about alternative approaches, and even innovating and testing new models, we are consequentially spending less time being productive in getting the job done as it is currently defined. But if our inventive time is successful, then we can bring our idea out to share with others, and spend our time being viewed as both productive *and* inventive. This relationship between inventive and productive time, as it plays out in the natural course of learning, is represented in the "Learning S-Curve" (see figure 6.2).

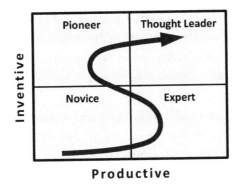

Figure 6.2—The Learning S-Curve

The Learning & Development leaders in most organizations have said many times that they strive to develop their staff "from novice to expert." But is an *expert* really the highest level of intellectual achievement? Business leaders today understand that they are either becoming Thought Leaders or they are becoming obsolete. If you are just an Expert, your job is about to be outsourced or embedded in a microchip. Once a performance improvement consultant interviews you and captures your decisions and procedures, they won't teach it to new novices, they will encode it into the workflow logic so that a novice can step though the process online and perform the work as well as an expert.

The Learning S-Curve shows us that learning is not 1-dimensional, from Novice-to-Expert, based on productivity alone. Inventiveness is also part of the fundamental feedback that drives learning. This creates the 2-dimensional matrix underlying the Learning S-Curve, which shows that beyond the Novice and Expert, we must also acknowledge the Pioneer and Thought Leader. The problem is that most organizations operate from a poor definition of *learning*, using a 1-dimensional view (Novice-to-Expert). The entire organization's job levels, pay levels, incentives, development plans, etc. are based on this idea. Most annual assessments for employee "potential" are based on the *confidence* found in an Expert, and not on the *questions* found in a Pioneer. Ironically, most companies usually require associates to sign documents that essentially say that any ideas they come up with while on the job will become intellectual property that belongs to the company. Yet at the same time, companies rarely provide any development beyond "novice to expert" or adequate support for "pioneer time."

We love to cherish the products and celebrate the success of Thought Leaders. But somehow we forget, for example, that the inventor of the 3M Post-it Note was once a Pioneer, being told to work on glues that *stick* instead of playing with glues that *don't* stick. Imagine, in a downward economy, he could have been laid off and we would all still be using paperclips. The organizations that know how to foster and measure inventive learning will be the ones known as the next Thought Leaders. It takes more than inviting a creativity speaker for the day. It will take systemic changes related to how the organization views change, learning, and leadership, as described in the three parts of this book. And it will take changes related to our economic theories related to the *source* of learning itself.

The classical economic theory called "Learn by Doing," attributed to the economist Kenneth Arrow, was based on his observation of Industrial Age (second industrial revolution) manufacturing workers' ability to increase their productivity through repetitive operations. The problem with this term as used in organizations today is that it is misconstrued to assume that if someone is *doing* something then they will also be *learning*. Yet it is possible, and maybe even probable, that many workers are busy *reactively* doing something all day long without any learning taking place. While "doing" and "trying" may look the same to some people, "doing" is primarily what happens in the half-pipe — "trying" is primarily what happens in the full-cycle. This Second Industrial Revolution economic theory needs to be updated for the Fourth Industrial Revolution, which I simply call "Learn by Trying."

Becoming a Thought Leader requires spending some time as a Pioneer, and there are *fears* related to this period of time. It requires risk-taking on the part of the individual, who was recently seen as the Expert who knows the answers but now seems unsure. There is a fear of failure in not emerging as a Thought Leader. There is a fear of not being sure about outcomes, but also doubts about your own abilities when you are used to being sure of yourself. As an Expert, we are able to speak with authority, with a voice of confidence, and this has led towards promotions into leadership. But when our productive work is falling behind, while we try new ideas that don't initially work, we may even fear for losing our job.

There are also fears within HR departments related to the Pioneer. We are not exactly sure how to measure and reward a pioneer. Should it be based on attempts or time spent? There is confusion about how to define "performance" as well as "potential" when comparing employees. Should Pioneers be rewarded for taking risks and trying new things? If so, at what point do rewards stop when no new good ideas emerge? What if the performance measurement process is designed to push the innovative people out of the organization to become an entrepreneur? There are clearly fears about the Pioneer from the individual as well as the organization.

To alleviate these fears, some people simply hide their Pioneer work from others, working overtime and on weekends. If their ideas do not work out then no one has to know, and they have not fallen behind in their expected productive work. But if they are successful, they appear to magically emerge from Expert directly to a Thought Leader. Sadly, another way that some avoid these fears altogether is to play it safe and keep their job, while never creating the inventions that we could all benefit from. Pioneering involves risk-taking so some may think it is *safe* to stop their development as an Expert. But in today's environment, we need to understand that it is also a risk to *not* strive towards becoming a Thought Leader. Staying where you are at is also risk-taking.

Variations of the Curve

There are two main variations to the normal Learning S-Curve, called the Sweeping S-Curve and the Narrow S-Curve (see figure 6.3). With the Sweeping S-Curve, you have an *entrenched* expert, that is used to being the person with the answers. They will need to learn how to have confidence in the questions—not just the answers. In many cases they are too deeply rooted in their identity as an Expert and may not be able to "make the turn" towards becoming a Pioneer. But if they can make the turns in the Sweeping S-Curve, they will be able to bring a richer set of connections into the process of creating new models.

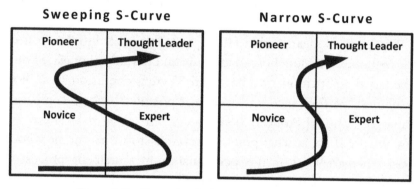

Figure 6.3—Sweeping S-Curve vs. Narrow S-Curve

With the Narrow S-Curve, you have cases where people appear to become an overnight success. Sometimes a Novice can come into an organization and be unaware of *entrenched thinking* that is holding them back, so they are bold enough to suggest or try ideas that others have thought will not work because for some reason they did not work in the past.

A Novice, or new person in an organization, may also bring existing knowledge from prior organizations to use as an analogy which could have the same effect of reaching Thought Leadership fairly quickly. Organizations tend to focus on "exit" interviews with employees when they leave. But "entry" interviews are also important if we consider the value of "fresh eyes." We need to view the novice, and the opportunity to be a novice, in new ways that appreciate the role for the value that unentrenched thinking brings, instead of assuming a novice in a new role brings no knowledge from prior experiences. As Klaus Schwab says in his book, *The Fourth Industrial Revolution*, "Given the increasing rate of change of technologies, the fourth industrial revolution will demand and place more emphasis on the ability of workers to adapt continuously and learn new skills and approaches within a variety of contexts."

Points Along the Curve

While moving through the Learning S-Curve, there are three key points along the way (see figure 6.4). At P1, we have a turning point, away from becoming a deeper Expert, and towards becoming a Pioneer. There is some doubt about the current model, and your curiosity could either lead to Thought Leadership or lead back to P1 with less doubt about the current model. All the way towards P2, the "what-if" type questions push the advancement within the S-curve, thinking that there may be a better way. Maybe you will find something as a new answer while still holding on to the current solution. Finding a "best practice" that someone else has used would allow you to retreat back, to be an Expert, now with an additional approach that you can use. But sometimes, you don't find an answer that easily, and you have to decide how important this endeavor is to you, because now the question has become a quest.

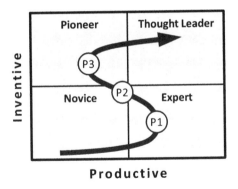

Figure 6.4—Learning S-Curve Points

At P2, the center of the S-curve, we have the inflection point. In the field of mathematics, this is the point within a curve that defines change. This is when the quest to find a new answer is stronger than the security of holding on to the old answer. This is like letting go of one side of the flying trapeze and moving through the air towards the other side, without having it in sight, and hoping that something is there to grab hold of before momentum and resources are gone. At P2, you are committed, not to an answer, but to a question. A decision has been made that whatever is found going forward has to be better than operating under the current model. There is no turning back— only going forward into the unknown. Now, as an early Pioneer, there is more exploring than there is creating. But you know that at some point soon you will need to grab hold of an idea you can believe in, which will allow you to turn the next corner in your journey.

At P3, we have a turning point, where your curiosity as a Pioneer is surpassed by your conviction towards a specific new idea. Performing original thinking is what happens here, which may or may not produce an original idea. It could be that someone else has beat you to the patent office with an idea that is similar to yours or even just like yours. If this happens, you can just give up on Pioneer time completely, or keep at it, knowing that one day, your original thinking will also produce an original idea. But if you find that your idea is unique, at least within your field, your company, and your team, then you can begin to create it, test it, and show it to others to get feedback as well as support.

After P3, productivity and progress towards Thought Leadership begins to accelerate as you "turn the corner" and are able to sound like a Pioneer with a positive vision, instead of the Pioneer that is still searching. Crossing the line, from Pioneer to Thought Leader, is a matter of perception. If someone else you know begins to adopt your new idea, then you have crossed the line. From here, your impact as a Thought Leader is just a matter of additional visibility, which takes time, and may take a lifetime, and may even take beyond your lifetime.

Developing Learners

Talent Management within our organizations requires a plan for business continuity and also a plan for continuing to challenge individuals. In making development decisions, it helps to also think about where each employee is at within the Learning S-Curve, and then support their development throughout the learning matrix (see figure

6.5). There are three primary ways to navigate within the story thinking cycle, and each of these three are important for supporting the development of knowledge workers:

- HPL: Half-Pipe Learning (Learning known/provided Answers and Procedures)
- PBL: Problem-Based Learning (Full-Cycle Learning with Disruption as a Problem)
- OBL: Opportunity-Based Learning (Full-Cycle Learning with Disruption as an Opportunity)

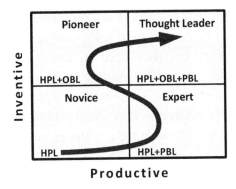

Figure 6.5—Developing Learners in the Learning S-Curve

Novice: The *Novice* requires Half-Pipe learning, that is, Education & Training, with Drill & Practice, to become oriented to the subject. Of course, it is theoretically possible for a pure Novice, with enough time, to learn the basics through their own trial and error. But in today's complex world, there is probably not enough time to become a Thought Leader in your lifetime without the kick-start of an education that hands you the knowledge of what is already known. Besides, even Beethoven started off by practicing the scales, and Isaac Newton said: "If I have seen further than others, it is by standing upon the shoulders of giants." Developing a novice typically involves on-boarding training and access to best-practice materials.

Expert: The *Expert* requires Half-Pipe learning, plus Problem-Based Learning. Expertise is more than memorizing the answer; it requires solving problems that come up when what used to work now won't work. This means going over the top, and asking questions required for inspection. And it means being very familiar with the current ways to manage the existing model for how things should work. From this ability, the right questions can be asked to solve a given problem. This entire cycle starts in the Disruption phase, where a given disruption is treated as a problem, not an opportunity. Developing an expert requires attending and speaking at targeted conferences, time and recognition for problems solved, and access to visualization and statistical tools.

Pioneer: The *Pioneer* requires Half-Pipe learning, plus Opportunity-Based Learning. Like the Expert, a Pioneer needs to know how to travel over the top, but they need to ask questions required for exploration, using *Appreciative Inquiry* techniques instead of just problem-solving techniques. This entire cycle starts in the Disruption phase, where a given disruption is treated primarily as an opportunity, not just a problem. Developing a pioneer requires attending and speaking at broader conferences (maybe not even directly related to their work), time and recognition for discoveries, and access to creativity tools. They may even struggle as they transition from the expert with the answers to the pioneer with the questions. But "pioneer time" should be a regular event, like Friday afternoon playtime, or a sabbatical for those with more tenure.

Thought Leader: The *Thought Leader* requires Half-Pipe learning, plus Opportunity-Based Learning, plus Problem-Based Learning— they need to put it all together. Before the inventor of the 3M Post-it Note became a thought leader, he had to solve a problem: A swipe of this new glue on a paper note worked better than using paperclips. Developing a thought leader requires attending broad conferences, presenting their ideas, and finding additional uses for their ideas. Emerging as a thought leader requires keeping up with research in their field, finding opportunities for improvement, and clearly aligning new solutions to real problems. But to fully develop a thought leader will require a deeper understanding of how *leadership* itself is affected by story thinking—enjoy Part III: Leadership.

Your Turn

Picture the Learning S-Curve as you work through the tasks below:

- For your organization, identify how all four learner types are measured and developed, and see if you can improve these processes.
- When in a *knowledge sharing* session in your organization, don't just talk about what you are doing that works, share what you are thinking about that does not yet work. Share your thoughts from all four learner types.
- It is helpful in our development to be truthful to ourselves and explicit with others when we are acting within each learner type. Some of us may be an expert within some field or domain, yet still be a novice within many others. Complete the statements below by filling in the blanks, and then think about the development you may need to reach the next level:
  - o I am seen as a novice within the field of _____ because _____.
  - o I am seen as an expert within the field of _____ because _____.
  - o I am seen as a pioneer within the field of _____ because _____.
  - o I am seen as a thought leader within the field of _____ because _____.

III

PART III: LEADERSHIP

7

Leading
Learning Organizations

"The only real sustainable solution is a real learning organization." — John Lewis

Q: What is the relationship between leading and learning?

Learning Organizations

While Arie de Geus was working at Royal Dutch/Shell as the head of the company's strategic planning group, he asked a powerful question which led to him becoming known as the "father of organizational learning." He was researching corporate longevity and wanted to know why the average life expectancy of a Fortune 500 firm is only 40 to 50 years. In this famous study, he found that the few longstanding companies had one thing in common—they had a view of their organization as a *living system* which can learn and grow to transcend beyond what they currently do (de Geus, 1997). This required more than training programs—it required a sense of identity beyond an institution for financial purposes. His conclusion was that organizations that cannot learn will not survive.

In his book, *The Fifth Discipline: The Art & Practice of The Learning Organization*, Peter Senge expands on the work of de Geus, and describes the disciplines needed for a *learning organization*, so that everything that has been learned *about* learning becomes the foundational base of the organization. This creates an agile organization that is more flexible and sustainable, by constantly learning, changing, and innovating beyond legacy products and services (see figure 7.1).

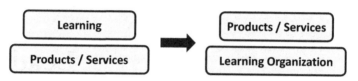

Figure 7.1—Learning Organization

Some leaders think that learning only occurs "down in the training department." Their mental model of the organization is based on the activities around their current products and services. Individual learning and training may occur on top of this base, and some organizational learning and knowledge sharing may occur as well, with learning primarily existing as an "add-on" to their primary work. But Senge's view of the organization places learning at the *base* of their primary work. He emphasizes the critical importance of learning within an organization—that it "may be the only sustainable competitive advantage."

So why, after several decades, do we not see more *learning organizations* popping up everywhere across the landscape? Senge also provides the answer to this question: "*Fragmentation, or making learning an 'add-on' to people's regular work, has probably limited more organizational learning initiatives than any other factor*" (Senge, 2006). The problem is that people see their "regular work" through the lens of "worker" steps, and see *learning* as an "add-on" to the work. By replacing an organization's primary operational model with one that is based on the foundations of story-based learning, then learning is not an "add-on" to business, but the *way* of business.

The key to establishing a learning organization is to fundamentally operate from a learning-based business model—and this is what story thinking provides. When you visualize your organization, what do you see? Do you picture a building, or a logo, or an organization chart?

Instead, visualize your organization as a working example of story thinking. Every conversation, decision, transaction, and project happens somewhere in the story thinking cycle. With the dispersed team members working in the fourth industrial revolution, this becomes the only common operational model for the organization.

Learner Leadership

Who gets to be the leader? At one time, we would say that "might makes right," meaning the leader was the strongest physically. But now when we get to *choose* our leaders, we usually try to look for people that know more than we do. For example, if we are travelling to Africa to see giraffes, who would we look for to lead us? We would want a safari guide, but also a safari guide with specific knowledge that will lead us in the right direction and keep us safe. How did they get this knowledge? Did they read a book before offering to lead us, or did they learn from experience over time? These are the same questions we have for the leaders of our organizations. The problem is that when selecting a leader, we tend to confuse their confidence with their capability.

Bertrand Russell said, "The trouble with the world is that the stupid are cocksure and the intelligent are full of doubt." Now known as the Dunning–Kruger effect, based on their studies in this area, the less capable people rate their own abilities above the average, while the competent rate their own abilities below the average (Dunning, 2011). It is about our ability to be "ignorant of our own ignorance." Those who have less ability to understand a topic can also have less ability to understand that there is no reason for them to be so confident about leading others. This is why I say that "the *real* problem with stupidity is that it doesn't stop at the doorstep of self-assessment."

This is not to say that an incompetent person will always remain inadequate. We are born as learners and continue learning and developing over time. The problem is that as we are developing our desire and ability to *understand*, and also developing our desire and ability to *influence* others, these learner-leadership capabilities rarely develop at the same rate (see figure 7.2).

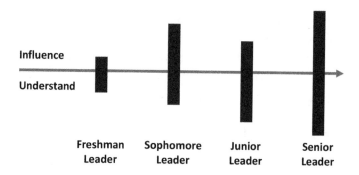

Figure 7.2—Learner Leadership: Influence vs. Understanding

Given the non-linear growth patterns between our desire to *influence* versus our desire to *understand*, as shown in the diagram above, we see that the "Sophomore Leader" emerges early as the leader in many organizations due to their leadership confidence. We can think of *influence* as the branches of a tree, above the ground, and think of *understanding* as the roots of a tree, below the ground. If a tree grows too fast before it has an appropriate root system, then a storm or situation it is unprepared for will be dangerous for the tree, and also dangerous for the leader as well as the organization.

The growth progression includes "growth pains" as the Learner Leader moves to each higher class. As the Sophomore Leader realizes that they may not know as much as they thought they did, they may sign-up for a master's degree, and the required extra time studying will make them less visible as an influencer. In many organizations, there are very knowledgeable people operating as "Junior Leaders" that know the most about running the organization, even though they are not at the top of the organization chart. Finally, the "Senior Leader" is the Learner Leader that realizes their visible leadership is needed as much as their knowledge, and they are willing to go through the growth pains and vulnerability of expanding their influence to match their deep knowledge which needs to be shared. But when it comes to the fourth industrial revolution, Klaus Schwab sees a need for more Senior Leaders, saying, "the required levels of leadership and understanding of the changes underway, across all sectors, are low when contrasted with the need to rethink our economic, social and political systems" (Schwab, 2017).

In their book, *Leading with the Future in Mind: Knowledge and Emergent Leadership*, Bennet, et al. summarize the progression of our concept of leadership: from physical strength as power – to knowledge as power; from hierarchy as authority – to knowledge as authority; from position defining the leader – to learning defining the leader; and from competition as influence – to collaboration as influence. Leadership today is related to learning as much as it is related to influence. Yet sadly, some people in the role of leadership are not interested in researching a topic (Investigation) before sharing their beliefs (Ideation), or changing their opinion based on new learnings in fear of looking indecisive. This pattern will continue until the followers of leaders embrace the expectation of the Leader as a Learner, able to influence through knowledge from anywhere within the hierarchy of an organization.

Leading Conversations

Learner Leaders must be able to balance their time being a transformational leader and also a transactional leader. And they need to communicate within two primary types of conversations: dialogue and directive. The leader is taking in information and including others in the dialogue, and then at some point the leader has to make a decision and deliver a directive which they expect others will follow. Both the dialogue and directive are needed. It is not a question as to which one is better, or which one is not required. The question is about how the leader balances these two primary types of conversations, and more importantly, how the leader communicates to others which forum they are working within. Without a round table (indicating equal status) that can transform so there is a clear head of the table (indicating rank), clearly communicating this transition can be a challenge.

Imagine a team leader saying, "I have an idea; what do you think of it?" Then a team member says, "OK, I will get right on that" (thinking that the leader brought this topic up for a reason beyond just talking about it). This is a case where the leader did not make it clear that they just wanted to share an idea and get feedback as well as other ideas. In this case, the leader should "over-communicate" and say: "I really just want your ideas right now." The problem is that some leaders are not clear about when the forum is a dialogue versus a directive. Sometimes the leader is only seen as providing directives, in which case the organization will simply shut down and not feel it is safe to offer ideas. Ultimately, fear of insubordination hurts the development of a learning culture, and it must be managed by the leader.

One way to separate dialogue and directive is to separate them in space and time. On one day, possibly at a site that is remote from normal operations, the team is engaged in dialogue and brainstorming. The next week, the leader can hold a meeting to present the new direction to the team. If the team and leader cannot get in sync, the leader can try a bold move and create a forum context sign that says either "Dialogue" or "Directive," much like a military meeting content sign that says "Classified" or "Unclassified." It needs to be just this clear at any given time. The leader is responsible for this clarity, but first needs to recognize the type of forum they are already operating within, and they will find that it is based on the types of questions being asked.

Sometimes I get a question that sounds like someone is just trying to *confirm* something, rather than *learn* something. You may have heard of these questions as the "have you stopped beating your wife" question. These are questions coming from a conviction rather than from a curiosity. So now when I get a question like this, I like to respond back with this question: "Are you asking me a question from curiosity or a question from conviction?" Sometimes it is not just the question but the way it is asked, that lets others know if you really want to learn or if you already have your mind made up.

The social forums we find ourselves within are based on whether our questions are coming from curiosity or from conviction (see table 7.1). For example, the forum is called *collaboration* when the participants are asking questions from curiosity, but the forum is called *groupthink* when the participants are asking questions from conviction. Consider the forums and question types in the table below:

Forum Type	Participant 1	Participant 2
Dialogue	Curiosity for Ideas	Curiosity for Ideas
Collaboration	Curiosity for Solutions	Curiosity for Solutions
Deliberation	Curiosity for Decision	Curiosity for Decision
Directive	Conviction of Prescriptive	Curiosity for Prescriptive
Education	Conviction of Descriptive	Curiosity for Descriptive
Persuasion	Conviction of Opinion	Curiosity for Opinion
Groupthink	Conviction of A	Conviction of A
Debate	Conviction of A (cognitive)	Conviction of B (cognitive)
Altercation	Conviction of A (emotion)	Conviction of B (emotion)

Table 7.1—Forum Type based on Curiosity and Conviction

A *debate* is a type of competition, where participants are working from conviction, not curiosity. But if both sides stand to gain from the correct decision, it should be conducted as a *collaboration*, where both sides are working from curiosity. The problem is that winning the debate becomes more important than winning the issue. People don't even know how to conduct themselves in a *deliberation* or *dialogue*, because there is very little to model after. The forums on many news networks are either *groupthink* or various forms of *altercation*.

I once worked with a leader that only knew how to ask questions from conviction—never from curiosity. He never realized that he was always creating a forum in every meeting where we could not collaborate or have a dialogue. Every question he asked sounded like an inquisition: "Isn't it true that you...?" Every answer from other people sounded defensive to explain how the opening question is not true, or at least, is not the best starting point for understanding the situation. This communication style comes from an older view of leadership, which may temporarily help the leader look like they are in charge, but the organization suffers in the long run by not engaging in true dialogue and collaboration towards the best solutions. It is also a communication style that may define a Sophomore Leader.

Daniel J. Boorstin is quoted as saying, "The greatest obstacle to discovery is not ignorance—it is the illusion of knowledge." I believe he was describing the very point in time when questioning from curiosity switches to become questioning from conviction. This is when we stop trying to learn and start trying to confirm. This is the "tipping point" in all of understanding. By being aware of the underlying question types that are driving our forums, a learner leader can change the questions from conviction to curiosity—and change the forum into dialogue and collaboration.

Knowledge Management

If you are in the Education & Training business, then there is no separation between knowledge level and organizational role level. An expert is higher in the organization, and is paid higher than the novice. And the job is about moving *people* through the system, while measuring progress against the single dimension of novice-to-expert.

If you are in the Knowledge Management (KM) business, it is not just about *who* the expert is—it is about knowing *where* expert knowledge resides, and finding the best ways to cultivate and leverage it within the organization. It is about moving *knowledge* through the system, which may *include* Education and Training, but this is not usually the sole solution. It usually includes systems to support inventive and productive feedback, and *embedding* expert knowledge into a job-aid, online form, workflow system, expert system, decision system, robot, or some other form of artificial intelligence (AI).

Leadership teams are not only simply *using* the information that they find within KM systems, their competitiveness is also related to their ability to *design* and integrate systems into their organization. Leadership teams are increasingly responsible for the effectiveness of KM strategies and systems (see figure 7.3) to ensure that organizational learning is occurring, and that knowledge is being created, captured, organized, shared, and leveraged throughout the internal and extended organization. This includes requirements for transactional half-pipe activities and also transformational full-cycle activities.

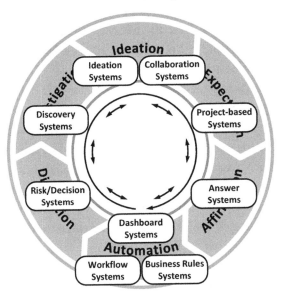

Figure 7.3—Knowledge Management Systems

We see both of these fundamental ways to answer questions within the knowledge systems used in our organizations. For example, a company will have a Web site with "authoritative" answers, usually in the form of FAQ (Frequently Asked Questions), where customers can find the definitive answer to their question. Companies do not want to provide customers access to their internal "collaboration" system, where several people and departments are involved in providing their opinion and rationale for the best authoritative answer for their customers.

Systems that support authoritative answers have progressed to allow many customers to find the answer to their question themselves, in a "self-service" system, rather than needing to call and talk to a person in a "call center" at a company. And systems that support the collaboration of ideas have progressed to allow for many more ideas from diverse groups to be considered and tracked.

Sometimes we find a hybrid system that does not try to find the authoritative answer or the collaborative online environment, but will try to find "an authority" on the subject, as an "Expert Finder" type of system. But these are systems designed from the premise that we need to ask the question "who" because answers to "what" and "why" will not or cannot be found directly.

As the demands increase for transparency into the decision-making process, the "Expert Finder" systems will be used less as an authoritative output and more as an input into who should be participating in the collaborative environment. In addition to finding technological progress with authoritative and collaborative systems, as separate systems, we will see progress in how they integrate into a single merged system. At this point, the KM systems not only *support* the enterprise strategy, they are able to *drive* the enterprise strategy.

Imagine reading an FAQ on a company Web site and calling to complain that the answer does not consider your situation. Imagine a worker in the call center clicking on that authoritative answer to indicate that it should be reviewed. Imagine the executives involved in making that decision getting notified that there may be a condition they did not consider when making that decision, and their entire decision logic appears for them to re-review. Imagine the transparency in the decision-making process when you, as the customer, are notified automatically that the authoritative answer has been updated. The development of KM systems has evolved somewhat in isolation but are moving more towards integration.

Cultural KPIs

One way to view organizations is that *some* are *learning* organizations, and *some* are *not*. Another way to view organizations, and the way I now prefer, is to acknowledge that *all* humans are born as learners who may need to overcome some learning disabilities. So, similarly, *all* organizations are *learning* organizations, with some having more learning disabilities than others. With this perspective, each organization can be surveyed and measured against Cultural Key Performance Indicators (KPIs) related to an effective learning organization. Below is an example assessment, which shows the relationship between each measurement and the phases within the story thinking cycle (see figure 7.4).

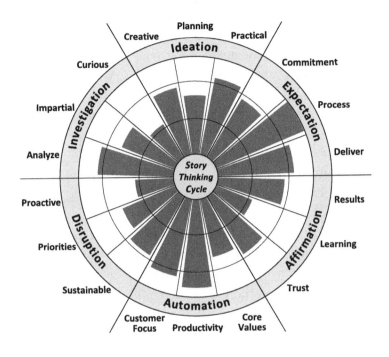

Figure 7.4—Cultural Key Performance Indicators (KPIs)

Peter Senge tells us that the leader's role is to create learning organizations (Senge, 1990). This will require the leader understanding themselves as a Learner Leader; this will require the leader recognizing the organization as a learning organization; and this will require a learning-centric view into how knowledge is managed, and learning is communicated in the organization.

Your Turn

Picture the Learner Leadership, Knowledge Management, and KPI models as you work through the tasks below:

- For your current field of study, complete the statements below by filling in the blanks, and then think about the development you may need to reach the next level:
  - o I am seen as a Freshman Leader within the field of _____ because _____.
  - o I am seen as a Sophomore Leader within the field of _____ because _____.
  - o I am seen as a Junior Leader within the field of _____ because _____.
  - o I am seen as a Senior Leader within the field of _____ because _____.
- In your next discussion or meeting, identify the type of forum you are in, and if needed, change the questions from conviction to curiosity to change the type of forum.
- Within your organization, write down the names of the technical platforms and systems you use as they align with the six phases of story thinking, and identify any gaps within the cycle.
- Use the Cultural KPI questions below (see table 7.2) to rate your organization against each Key Performance Indicator (KPI) between 1 and 10 (1 means poor capability and 10 means extremely strong capability):

Rate: 1-10	Cultural KPIs	Description
	Creative	Teams incorporate brainstorming and diversity of initial ideas while individuals are encouraged to "think outside the box" for solutions
	Planning	Team members understand a shared vision and strategy, including risks and rewards, and error preference of tradeoff decisions
	Practical	New ideas balance ingenuity with attainability, given deadlines and current capabilities of people, process, and technology

	Commitment	Team members are fully committed to the goals, within a culture that allows for new strategies instead of sticking with a "bad" plan
	Process	Project methodologies provide clear expectations and development processes, and ongoing progress is communicated to stakeholders
	Deliver	Project deliverables meet or exceed customer expectations for quality, quantity, cost, and timeframe
	Results	Interactions produce positive "win-win" outcomes and lasting relationships for all involved, external and internal stakeholders
	Learning	Team members learn equally from internal lessons, best practice research, and customer feedback, without need to relearn
	Trust	Authoritative answers are easily found, and trusted, and adequate transparency and oversight ensures confidence in the answers
	Core Values	Organizational values are known and practiced by team members, and are designed into operational practices
	Productivity	Operational activities are efficient and effective, using a balance of training and automation systems, towards stated metrics
	Customer Focus	Operational activities are centered primarily around the customer, with reasonable decision escalation timelines being met
	Sustainable	Appropriate monitoring, countermeasures, and maintenance is practiced throughout the human/technology working environment
	Priorities	Opportunities and problems are prioritized and communicated, based on importance, urgency, impact, effort, and constraints
	Proactive	Team members routinely identify risks, and create strategies to predict, prevent, prepare, or preempt larger issues
	Analyze	Team members rely on systems thinking and statistical analysis for root factors and root causes, before suggesting solutions
	Impartial	Team members seek grounded research by reframing initial assumptions and questions, and addressing bias and groupthink
	Curious	Discovery of new possibilities is rewarded, and operationalized via designated "pioneer time" to explore a broad range of interests

Table 7.2—Cultural KPI Survey Questions

8

Leading with Transparency

"A lack of transparency results in distrust and a deep sense of insecurity." — Dalai Lama

Q: How can we build transparency instead of just trying to build trust?

Consequential Knowledge

I have come to realize that there is one specific move that is made by every chess player, at some point in their life, which is a move that is not found in instructional books for how to play chess. This is the move where the chess player holds their finger on top of the chess piece and announces: "I am still touching it!" Why are they so careful about letting go? They understand that when they let go of that chess piece that the current list of options will consequentially move into a new set of options, and they can't go back.

Business and policy decisions work the same way. We like to think of them as individual questions and answers, but in reality, our current decisions are based consequentially from previous decisions. Within story thinking, to answer the question "why" we need to connect all the individual questions and answers for each of the six phases, and show the options that were chosen, but also the options *not* chosen.

Decisions are made daily at every level within an organization, *presumably* within the context of prior decisions. But this is a big presumption. With higher amounts of personnel turnover, and little documentation, we have less corporate memory. At its core, business is about making decisions and learning from those decisions. While the factors into our choices are becoming more complex, we find we are required to make reflective decisions even faster, while needing to leave a trail of our thinking for the sake of transparency, which is increasingly demanded. "Decision-makers from all parts of global society seem to be in a state of ever-increasing exhaustion, so deluged by multiple competing demands that they turn from frustration to resignation and sometimes despair" (Schwab, 2017). With expectations for decreased product development cycle times, and increased innovation, the questions we ask are key, as are the tools we use to keep track of the decisions we make, and options considered.

For most of the questions we ask, we currently have tools that are ubiquitous—they are found everywhere, and most people know how to use them. We take for granted that everyone knows what a *map* and *calendar* are, and that they have become integrated expectations of a modern life. We have visual tools to help us answer questions related to "where" (map), "when" (calendar), "who" (organization chart), and "how" (process map), but not for "why." We rely on structured tools such as calendars, day planners, checklists, and to-do lists for daily work because they prove more reliable than our memory. Yet during a *thought* process, whether in a project design meeting, a debate, instructional lesson, or team collaboration—we fail to use structured tools to help us remember what we are thinking *from*.

In recent times there has been an explosion in technologies around what we have called "social media." But this phenomenon is really just our movement towards new tools to help us answer the question "Who" with greater context. When it comes to the question of "Why," we find that the tools have not caught up with the other questions. An executive remarked "I used a contact list, calendar, watch, map, and GPS to get to a meeting where we sat around and discussed WHY, without the realization that we even needed any tools [for WHY]." The troubling realization is that the *most important* question is the *least supported*.

Option Outlines

Currently there are tools that help us answer the basic question of "which" when making a *single* decision, for example, by using a prioritization matrix with weighted importance assigned to specific requirements. And software exists to aid us when the number of variables going into a single decision reaches into the hundreds.

But there are few tools that help us answer the basic question of "why" when asking to see, in one snapshot, the *multiple* options and decisions that have led to the current situation. Projects end with choices made that were either not captured, or were buried somewhere within the prose of many documents. When an organized approach is attempted, we begin to see the structure of a *decision tree*, which lists *all* of the possible options and choices, instead of just the ones considered and needed at the time. But requiring *all* possible options to be documented has resulting in capturing *none* of them.

Instead of this "all or nothing" approach to seeing our options and choices, I created the Option Outline as a "decision canvas" to see just the *chosen branches* of a decision tree (introduced in *The Explanation Age*). I call this design an Option Outline because it uses the structure of an outline (see figure 8.1) but shows the thought process of the options considered at each step. It more-closely aligns with our decision-making process, where we quickly consider but then dismiss some options, without needing to complete that branch.

For example, let's say that I am told one morning that we can go out and eat at a restaurant that day, but I have to quickly choose which meal it's going to be and what I might order. If my first decision is based on the meal, then this decision will consequentially limit the follow-on options. So, let's compare a Decision Tree with an Option Outline for this example. Within the Option Outline, by reading from top to bottom, we see for each indentation the options considered, with the *chosen* option listed *last*.

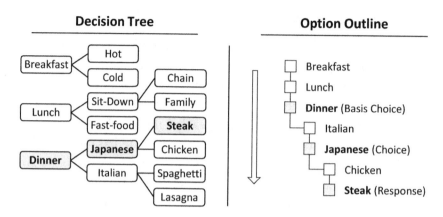

Figure 8.1—Decision Tree vs. Option Outline

The structure of an Option Outline allows us to quickly capture what options were considered, which option was chosen (listed last), and the entire consequential thought process (via indentation). Below is an Option Outline that shows us the thought process for deciding to use an Option Outline (see table 8.1).

Option Outline: Using an Option Outline	
Humans don't need to make complex decisions (basis: no problem)	↓
Humans <u>do</u> need to make complex decisions (basis: the problem)	(*Choice*)
Humans don't find tools helpful	↓
Humans <u>do</u> find tools helpful	(*Choice*)
Use special software	↓
Use decision tree diagrams	↓
Use <u>Option Outlines</u> (the solution)	(*Choice*)

Table 8.1—Using an Option Outline

The basis for any thought process, or where it starts, will be found in the top level of the Option Outline. In this case, the options we have listed are that humans either do our do not need to make complex decisions. Given we have listed the option that says we *do* need to make complex decisions *last*, this is our choice between these options, and we indent down to the next set of options that *must consequentially* be driven from the prior decision. In this case we choose that humans do find tools helpful, which leads us to the final consequential set of options to choose from, where we are choosing to use Option Outlines.

Studies have shown that students who make decisions while using "argument map" software perform better at critical thinking skills (Twardy, 2003). This should be as obvious as saying that people that drive while using a map or GPS perform better at navigation skills. But tools to support critical thinking skills are not regularly found within organizations, due to the inefficient "boxes-and-arrows" user interfaces requiring special software and wasted efforts completing unnecessary branches of thought. It is time for the Option Outline to become ubiquitous.

Let's look at an example Option Outline that you may use when buying a car (see table 8.2).

Option Outline: Buying a car	
Story Phases	Goal: Replace unreliable car and save money
Automation	Accept unreliable car as the status-quo
Disruption	The car will not pass inspection
Investigation	Fix the old car
Investigation	Buy a replacement car
Investigation	Get a new car
Investigation	Get a used car
Ideation	Gas car
Ideation	Electric car
Ideation	Hybrid car
Expectation	Purchase and collect data on savings

Table 8.2—Option Outline: Buying a Car

The Option Outline above shows the thought process of the options considered and the option chosen (listed last for each indentation) during each of the phases within the story thinking cycle. It is easy to quickly see why the car was purchased and the type that was chosen. Note that it is also easy to see the types of cars that were *not* considered as options, for example a diesel car was not considered. The Option Outline can help us visualize our options and choices within many personal settings. It has even been used within corrections facilities to help inmates, who are about to be released, to see how their decisions led to their situation, and how to map out future decisions. One corrections officer noted that "by using the option outline, it improved the offender's comprehension of his decisions by allowing him to visualize them, rather than just having to respond to his situation in a verbal discussion."

Now let's look at a business example. Don't you hate it when a lot of thought has gone into a final decision, and then there is this guy that comes in late to the process and belittles the decision with little understanding? Then what do you say? We usually say something like "a lot of thought has gone in to this," etc. Regardless of what we say, it doesn't seem to change minds or pass the transparency test. Instead, next time just show them the Option Outline you have created for the project.

Sometimes a Vice President in the organization sits in on a project meeting and makes a decision that will have consequences later on. The team that has been running the project makes it clear that there are better long-term choices, but their decision is overridden. A year later, when the project requires making some difficult choices, the same VP returns, demanding to know how the project could have gotten to the point where such bad choices are now the only options. In these cases, an Option Outline helps by pointing to the earlier option recommended and the one that they chose which has consequentially put the project in the current situation. Below is an example of choosing a work project solution when there is not a perfect solution (see table 8.3).

Option Outline: Work Project – Why Solution Z Was Chosen		
Story Phases	**Goal: Find Solution to Work Project**	**Notes**
Automation	Accept current issues as the status-quo	*Links*
Disruption	Identify and prioritize the current issues	*Links*
Investigation	Custom programming would not be supported	*Links*
Investigation	Off-the-shelf software is supported but incomplete	*Links*
Ideation	Select vendor W, X, or Y	*Links*
Ideation	Select vendor Z (*Link to Decision Matrix*)	*Links*
Expectation	Wait for missing feature to be added	*Links*
Expectation	Add custom code for missing feature	*Links*
Expectation	Use manual temporary workaround	*Links*
Affirmation	It works but some complain about extra work	*Links*

Table 8.3—Option Outline: Work Project Decisions

The example above shows how Option Outlines are used online with hyperlinked *notes* for supporting data and decision rationale. Instead of reading through documents with lots of data, where the explanations may be buried or missing completely, now the explanation is the main interface and the data are embedded as associated links.

Most companies today have adopted a practice of documenting "lessons learned" at the end of key projects. But most companies today do not kick-off new projects by searching through any lessons learned because it would take too long due to the format in which lessons are documented. If the learnings were captured in the form of an Option Outline, with links to the reasons the decisions were made, then a kick-off meeting for a new project could easily include a search to see that something similar was tried in the past. Creating a "learning organization" has become more than just trying to learn *faster* than competitors, it is about *applying* learnings throughout the organization with efficiency, while providing transparency into the decisions made.

Program Summaries and Lessons Learned

In 2009, Richard Martin published a powerful example in *Wired* magazine of *not* having ready access to the thought process of previous projects. An engineer was recently thumbing through a book published in 1958 to learn more about the beginnings of atomic energy. Of course, we have all heard of *Plutonium* and *Uranium* for the role they play in nuclear weapons and nuclear energy. But buried inside this old book were the notes on another possible solution that was tested but discarded many years earlier, called *Thorium*.

Atomic research essentially began as a military project, and Thorium was just not the best choice for making a weapon—although its side effects are less risky. Now some believe it is the perfect material for safer commercial nuclear power plants. The purpose here is not to debate the final viability that Thorium may play for nuclear energy, as it is still being researched at this time, but to argue that an Option Outline could have been created that listed Thorium as an option not chosen, with links to supporting material which future research could have built upon more quickly.

What makes Thorium a Knowledge Management (KM) topic, and not just an energy topic? The answer is that Thorium is not a new discovery; it is a *re-discovery*. Over 70 years ago it was tested as part of the Manhattan Project. It was found to be safer and more abundant than Uranium, but it could not produce an atomic bomb, which was the purpose of the project. But after WWII, when commercial nuclear power plants were needed, consequential momentum led us to use the most dangerous material for the job. Over 70 years of lost knowledge was wasted towards other possible solutions—not to mention the accidents. Imagine a world without the disasters of Chernobyl and Fukushima.

Key project decisions, and the options considered, are currently not documented at all, or they are buried deep within various documents, to hopefully be rediscovered decades later. Instead, imagine having all of the key decisions listed on a single page for every project. In the case of the Manhattan Project and subsequent commercial projects, we can construct an Option Outline for nuclear age material decisions (see table 8.4).

Option Outline: Nuclear Age Material Decisions		
Story Phases	**Goal: Decide on Best Nuclear Material per Goal**	**Notes**
Automation	Let Nazi Germany build first nuclear weapons	*Links*
Disruption	Initiate the American Manhattan Project (choice)	*Links*
Investigation	Use Thorium (can't produce a bomb but safer/abundant)	*Links*
Investigation	Use Uranium (can produce Plutonium and a bomb)	*Links*
Ideation	Abandon nuclear technologies after WWII	*Links*
Ideation	Create nuclear energy plants	*Links*
Ideation	Use Thorium (not really considered)	*Links*
Ideation	Use Uranium (use what experts are familiar with)	*Links*

Table 8.4—Option Outline: Nuclear Age Material Decisions

Documenting project summaries is something that most do not do well, if at all. When "lessons learned" are actually documented, we write them as if their only use will be by someone in the future that wants to *repeat* the project exactly in its entirety. But just as valuable (as key decisions) is the knowledge of what options were *not* chosen for that project, because they could be the very options needed for a future project.

Your Turn

Picture the Option Outline and Story Thinking cycle as you work through the tasks below:

- For a given problem (you pick one) and solution, create an Option Outline that presents your thought process with at least four indentations to document your options and choices.

- Using standard presentation or word processing software, create an Option Outline with *hyperlinks* that lead to notes, supporting data, and rationale for choosing or not choosing an option.
- Ask to see someone's Option Outline, when they say they have an idea, to see if they have thought it through.
- Review your last big project or decision, and then map the key options and choices into an Option Outline, to create a program summary, and also see if you would have made different decisions by using an Option Outline.

9

Collaborative Policy-Making

"While all other sciences have advanced, that of government is at a standstill—little better understood, little better practiced now than three or four thousand years ago." — John Adams

Q: How should organizations and nations self-govern with transparency?

The Policy-Making Steps

"From now on, this is what we are going to do." This is how the introduction to a new policy usually begins. And most of us have heard a policy as children that sounded something like this: "From now on, bedtime will be 10 o'clock." OK, so some of you could stay up past midnight. The point is that a policy is something we are very familiar with in our homes, schools, and businesses. It is not something reserved just for the government policy "makers" that we call politicians. A policy is simply a mandated routine and status quo. In some cases, we might call it a rule or a law. So, most of us are familiar with what a policy is—but do we really understand how a policy is made? The *pure* process of policy-making (not politics) follows the sensemaking flow of story thinking (see figure 9.1).

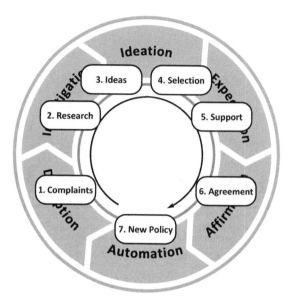

Figure 9.1—Policy-Making Full-Cycle Steps

It should be no surprise that the process of policy-making, in its natural form, follows the story thinking cycle. Regardless if the policy is for a home or business or nation, the steps are the same:

1. Complaints: Some person or interested group/party is dissatisfied with the status quo.
2. Research: We research to determine root causes and factors underlying the complaint.
3. Ideas: We generate improvement ideas for legitimate and prioritized complaints.
4. Selection: A specific improvement idea is selected (we submit a bill in congress**).
5. Support: The sponsor of the new idea looks to find support (votes) for the idea.
6. Agreement: The sponsor of the new idea finds/generates agreement (bill signed).
7. New Policy: The new routine (law) is operationalized.

** Note: Listing "Submit Bill" as "Step 1" is not logical.

We were taught that the first step in making a new law is to submit a bill, which is simply an idea to be considered towards the next mandated routine. But this step is the submission of a selected idea within Ideation among other ideas considered. What were those other ideas and why were they not selected? And this occurred after some root cause analysis within Investigation to determine the true problem which requires a solution. What research was performed and what were the other possible factors for the disruption? And this occurred after some complaints were made within Disruption about the current policy and status quo. Which organization or individuals made the complaint and how do their interests compare to those who have not made a complaint? What tradeoff decision within the current policy had to be made which we could have anticipated the source of complaints?

When it comes to "the people's" business, policy-making is mandatory—politics is optional. Yet without story thinking to provide a pure sensemaking process to compare with, politics becomes the norm. As governments increasingly are expected to operate *like* a business, the citizens will expect their institutions to operate as learning organizations with transparency into the policy-making process.

Problem Reaction Solution

In chapter one, we saw how story thinking is a process to get "from problem to solution." In some cases, we do not have full transparency into the process for changing our policies or mandated routines, and in other cases the process itself can become abbreviated or even manipulated. The German philosopher Georg W. F. Hegel described an abbreviated logic process (Maybee, 2016), now known as the "Hegelian Dialectic," with three parts: 1) the Problem or thesis, 2) the Reaction or antithesis, and 3) the Solution or synthesis (see figure 9.2).

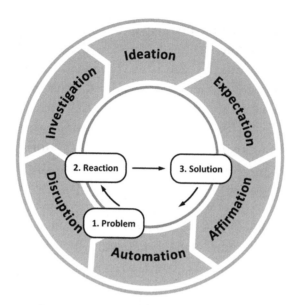

Figure 9.2—Policy-Making Half-Pipe Steps

This logic process is an *abbreviated* decision cycle in that it operates within the half-pipe instead of the full-cycle of story thinking. The upside of this logic process is that it is faster than thinking through the full-cycle, as the *solution* is expected to *alleviate* the tension between the problem and reaction, and not just supply an idea for consideration. The downside of this process is that it does not take the time to go through the full-cycle to investigate root causes or ideate several possible solutions. Because of this, it can be used to manipulate change by not providing time for reactive emotions to dissipate before a new ruling is pushed into place.

When used for manipulative purposes, the "Problem" is an outrageous event which is *created* by those in control, wishing to force a new mandated policy or law. The "Reaction" is the immediate emotional response expected of the public or targeted audience, which generally is outrage about the event and demand for change. With this emotionally-charged environment, the "Solution" is a new policy quickly pushed into place that was desired by the controlling authority, which has not had time to be thoughtfully reviewed or reconsidered by the public. In his book, *Media Control: The Spectacular Achievements of*

Propaganda, Noam Chomsky describes processes like the Hegelian Dialectic as a way to "manufacture consent."

Complex situations require reaching Ideation to be able to make a *tradeoff* decision, instead of settling for a *reactive* emotional decision. Any manipulative person, not just an authoritative government, can use this approach. For example, Munchausen Syndrome, also called Factitious Disorder, is when a person secretly harms themselves or their own children (problem) so that others respond with concern and kindness (reaction), so that they get the attention or other desires they crave (solution), no matter what it takes. When driven by a "We must act now!" mentality, there is a chance that the full-cycle is being short-circuited to keep our thinking within the half-pipe.

Also, by *not* performing expected procedures, maintenance, or precautionary measures, it ensures that eventually a "crisis" will emerge on its own which allows this technique to be used. If a problem is described as a "crisis" by an authoritarian, yet they were in the leadership role responsible for ensuring that a crisis did not occur, then there is a chance that "Problem, Reaction, Solution" is at play.

Transparent Policy-Making

In every business, policy-making requires the story thinking pattern to find the best tradeoffs in the rules that will drive routine. And as governments increasingly are expected to operate like a business, the citizens will expect their institutions to operate as learning organizations. In the previous chapter we learned about the Option Outline tool to help leaders keep track of their decisions while providing others with transparency into the decision-making process. Here we will use the Option Outline to help with transparency in the policy-making process.

Using the topic of climate change, given it is well known and sufficiently complex, we can follow the thinking of how a bill becomes a law, with an Option Outline. The purpose here is not to debate the solution of cap and trade, but to show how an Option Outline can help untangle a compressed thought process, to keep our own thinking straight and provide transparency for others.

Below is an Option Outline related to the problem of climate change with the solution of cap and trade (see table 9.1). I was not able to directly construct this Option Outline using "official" documents because they focus on describing "how" a new law would operate, not "why" we need a new law or "how" each choice was made. The purpose here was not to take any sides but to illustrate the value of seeing many opinions presented within a small outline. When opinion polls are taken on any of these options by themselves, they are essentially taken out of context from the overall thought process.

Option Outline: Climate Change		
Story Phases	**Goal: Support for Global Cap and Trade**	**Notes**
Automation	Earth temperature is within normal cycles (no problem)	*Links*
Disruption	Earth temperature is cooling (problem)	*Links*
Disruption	Earth temperature is warming (problem chosen to solve)	*Links*
Investigation	Measurements of CO2 level increase are flawed	*Links*
Investigation	Measurements of CO2 level increase are not flawed	*Links*
Investigation	Human activities have not caused global warming	*Links*
Investigation	Human activities have caused it, based on CO2 levels	*Links*
Investigation	Changes in human activities will not have an impact	*Links*
Investigation	Changes in human activates can solve problem	*Links*
Ideation	Build more nuclear power plants	*Links*
Ideation	Invest in electric cars and solar power	*Links*
Ideation	Create a market to trade carbon taxes	*Links*
Expectation	Push for a Cap and Trade bill in Congress	*Links*

Table 9.1—Option Outline: Example for Bills becoming Laws

If you favor the global cap and trade system, then you may agree with this Option Outline and can defend the choices. You can probably add other options that were considered, and defend an argument for how your thinking got from the problem of global warming to this idea for the solution. If, on the other hand, you do not favor this solution, you can probably create links to data in support of your choices, and list additional options that were not considered. The Option Outline provides a way to quickly become educated on the issues and options, and to find the weakest link in the chain of decisions that, if broken, will introduce doubt into the solution.

In his book, *The Goal*, Eliyahu Goldratt argues that by using a "Theory of Constraints," you can predict that the weakest link in any process will not only be the first to break, but it will break the entire process. So, we could also say that the weakest choice or argument within an Option Outline, when broken, will also break the entire chain of thought towards the final choice. And when this happens, we should know *where* most people disagree within the chain of an entire thought process, to begin questioning and communicating at that point.

For example, some people may be labeled as "global warming skeptics" when really they are skeptics of "man-made" global warming, or just skeptics of cap and trade as the best solution. An Option Outline lets us see exactly where within a thought process an agreement breaks down. In general, wherever we find disagreement of opinions, an Option Outline can be used for conflict resolution purposes to find where there is agreement and where that agreement breaks down. This will become increasingly important as "the fourth industrial revolution will affect the scale of conflict as well as its character. The distinctions between war and peace and who is a combatant and non-combatant are becoming uncomfortably blurred" (Schwab, 2017).

Professionals need a dashboard to make decisions. A pilot needs a dashboard to know the altitude, compass heading, fuel level, etc. And a business owner needs a business metrics dashboard. What does a citizen need to form his or her valuable opinion? Does a lengthy online document work? Can we be assured that a document would even include the decisions for *why* we need a new program, or would the document simply describe *how* the new program would work? Does an online opinion poll with icons for a "thumbs up" and "thumbs down" help us understand? Of course not. These are poor inputs into a thought process that has important outputs.

Imagine having an online system that connects all of the documents related to policy-making. Instead of just reciting the "law," we can click to find the original bill or court decision, what situations were considered—and even read the "dissenting" votes in a court opinion. Imagine being able to access each phase of the story thinking cycle related to any initiative. Then you can see if the actual bills and projects underway align with the prioritized issues identified in the Disruption phase. Imagine seeing an Option Outline that came out of an Ideation phase, with links to supporting material for why each option was chosen or not chosen. And imagine seeing the Affirmation phase for each chosen decision, with supporting material that shows if the idea is working or not.

The majority of the world's countries are now democratic. And with this dispersion of authority comes the responsibility of the citizens to discuss the ideas that govern their future. Instead of listening to debates between two sides of an issue, each side, to prove they were listening, should have to create an Option Outline that represents the other person's basis and train of thought. Then the two would have to work together to create a single Option Outline to show a basis they have in common, and where their conclusions begin to part ways. A visual debate will show us who is asking questions from curiosity, and who is asking questions from conviction. And the process will force us away from forums with conviction, towards forums with curiosity—from debate to dialogue.

For corporate business, and the people's business, imagine transparency measured by how clearly the thought process is presented, rather than how many documents are posted online. Seeking a thought process and finding only a final answer is like seeking a financial audit trail yet only finding a final tally. It's like travelling to watch a game and getting there in time just to see the final score. We look for answers in documents that are not designed to align with our sense-making process. The options and decision rationale are either buried or missing. Instead, imagine finding the logic flow, which follows the sensemaking pattern of story thinking, from which we can reach the data and details. The technical capabilities exist for this kind of access and insight into the policy-making process. The only thing missing is, you guessed it, a policy to make it happen.

Elegance of Policy-Making

Oliver Wendell Holmes once said, "I wouldn't give a fig for the simplicity on *this* side of complexity, but I would give my right arm for the simplicity on the *far side* of complexity." He was describing the *elegance* found only after having the knowledge of the options and choices considered throughout the story thinking cycle which have been boiled down to the basics of what to do (see figure 9.3).

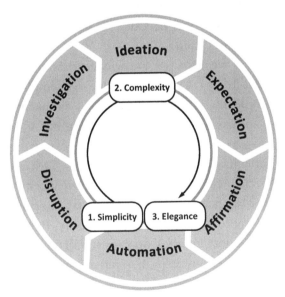

Figure 9.3—Simplicity vs. Elegance

Elegance is the wise simplicity, found on the *far* side of complexity. This is very different from the naive simplicity, found on *this* side of complexity. The problem is that to the novice, they sound the same, unless they are aware of this difference and understand the importance in asking the right questions. If we were in a tense situation, where we have ten seconds to defuse a bomb, and I tell you to cut the red wire, not the blue wire, what would you do? My instruction seems clear, but is my solution *simple* or *elegant*? Did I base it on a coin toss, or on years of experience in quickly recognizing bomb-making materials and methods?

Business operations, within the Automation phase of the story thinking cycle, are usually condensed procedures. There is rarely complete documentation on what the specific procedures are, relying instead on the memory of the individuals in the organization. So, there is usually no documentation connecting the procedures back to a thought process of options that were once considered. There will naturally be a group of people that assume the procedures represent *elegance*, and they will dutifully memorize them. We call them *Loyal New-Hires*. There will also naturally be a group of people that assume no procedures have been thought out, so all instructions represent *simplicity*. We call them *Teenagers*.

Note that when we lose the knowledge that created an elegant solution, all that is left is tradition and perceived simplicity. Without a memory of complexity, elegance sounds like simplicity. So, we will relearn lessons, and history will repeat itself, without an organizational goal to not allow elegance to become simplicity over time. When we fail, the next generation finds themselves within Disruption, and the story thinking cycle begins again. Education, Organizational Learning, and Knowledge Management are the fields that can possibly stop the knowledge erosion from elegance into simplicity, but we would first need to get better at documenting options and decisions, documenting lessons learned, and sharing them in a findable way.

Criticality of Policy-Making

Transparency International is an organization that tracks corruption and transparency measurements for each country around the globe. They have found that the governments with higher corruption are associated with the countries that have higher poverty rates. To turn this statement around, the governments with increased transparency are associated with the countries that have higher qualities of life. Transparency within the policy-making process is an indicator of how well the citizens will live. So, as we move into the fourth industrial revolution, "governments, in their current form, will be forced to change as their central role of conducting policy increasingly diminishes due to the growing levels of competition and the redistribution and decentralization of power that new technologies make possible" (Schwab, 2017).

Deeper than the concern for how well we live is the concern for if we live at all. Enrico Fermi, a famous physicist, looked at the enormity of the universe, the number of stars like our Sun, the probability of those stars having planets, and the possibility of life elsewhere in the universe. On the one hand, he had a very large number representing the probability of extraterrestrial life. Yet on the other hand, he had a number representing the confirmed contacts with extraterrestrial civilizations: zero. He famously asked: "Where is everybody?"

Now known as the Fermi paradox, many possible explanations have been provided by the scientific community. The main groups of ideas are that they are too far away in distance and technology; they don't want to talk to us right now; they are communicating but we don't know what to look for; and they are already here but are hiding.

Another way of answering this paradox was provided by Charles Krauthammer, a *political* scientist. His explanation was it is likely that "intelligent" life has probably annihilated itself. In his book, *Things That Matter*, he pointed out that from what we know about our own planet, as civilizations become more technologically advanced, they reach a point where they have the means to annihilate themselves. "A mere 17 years after Homo sapiens discovered atomic power, those most stable and sober states, America and the Soviet Union, came within inches of mutual annihilation" (Krauthammer, 2013). He argued that with all the genius ideas and advancements in each of the arts and sciences, civilizations still ultimately maintain sustainability through what is known as *politics*. "Everything else rests upon it. Fairly or not, politics is the driver of history."

Now, with several countries setting their sights on going to Mars, the hope is that as humans become multi-planet beings that humanity will have a better chance of survival. But in addition to taking our technologies with us to other planets, we will also be taking our limitations in how we work together. While bringing people together around a shared mission and vision is a great way to *begin* our work, it is not enough to provide sustainability *throughout* the work.

Story thinking allows us to see the *pure* sensemaking process in producing a *policy*—the new mandated routine. From this vantage point, *politics* is more easily identified as *corruption*, just as counterfeit currency is more easily identified by those who study authentic legal tender. And authoritarian simplicity is more easily identified by those who study the elegance found in transparency and tradeoffs. Story thinking is about *applied* and *shared* sensemaking, which brings social understanding to *change, learning,* and *leadership*. When humans do eventually leave Earth for other planets, it could well be that the most important thing we take with us is not our technology but our stories, documented in the structure of story thinking.

Your Turn

Picture the policy-making steps within the Story Thinking cycle as you work through the tasks below:

- Describe the last new policy made at home in terms of the 7 policy-making steps, and see if any steps were missed ("because I said so" is a typical way to skip steps).
- When provided with a new policy or ruling, seek for transparency into each of the seven steps.
- Use an Option Outline to help resolve a conflict of opinions by mapping out the combined thought logic and identifying the location where differences begin.
- For the rules and operating procedures within your organization, identify the ones that appear as simplistic, which provide no additional rationale, versus the ones that appear as elegant, where the memory of complexity is still findable within the organization.

Summary:
Applying Story Thinking

In summarizing the concepts presented in this book, six key principles are presented which cover the span of topics and support the task of applying story thinking within an organization:

Story-based Work: With story thinking, the mental model of *work* is not a "process;" it is a "story." Every conversation, decision, transaction, and project happens somewhere in the story thinking cycle. Don't just *describe* the work as a story, but instead *design* the work through agile navigation around the story thinking cycle for each stakeholder. For example, the customer may be in Disruption, but your company should be able to begin in Automation because dealing with such events is your normal routine. And the goal may not always be to reach a state of Automation, as Marketing strives to create a positive Disruption.

Positive Outlook: The story you design into your work should not be a tragedy. Seek the positive side of each story, and within each phase of the story thinking cycle. For example, within Disruption, the problem can be an opportunity; and within Investigation, the questions can be based on appreciative inquiry. An overall positive outlook towards sustainability also emerges for teams, given reduced decision cycle times from the shared mental model of story thinking.

Transparent Decisions: In complex organizations, we need to keep track of our decisions to remember our rationale and to provide transparency. Using an Option Outline is one way to visually record options and choices made throughout the story thinking cycle. Complex situations require "tradeoff" decisions within Ideation which produce expected events in Disruption. For example, if we would rather err on the side of letting a guilty person go free than to condemn an innocent person, then we can expect a guilty person to occasionally go free.

Symbiotic Sensemaking: Instead of just looking for the "IF/THEN" in causal sensemaking, look for the "AND" in symbiotic sensemaking. If there is a problem, then look for the opportunity. If there are directions, then look for the map. For your given perception, consider your perspective. Within today's reality, look for tomorrow's vision. Story thinking is more than agile and cyclic events; it includes "at the same time" relationships.

Lifelong Learning: We are born as learners. But educational pedagogy and repetitive jobs can turn us into "knowers" that have become stuck in the half-pipe of the story thinking cycle. A commitment to lifelong learning requires developing from a novice to an expert, but also continuing as a pioneer towards becoming a thought leader. And it also may require embracing opportunities to become a novice again, in a new job or field of study.

Learner Leadership: As we are developing our desire and ability to *understand*, and also developing our desire and ability to *influence* others, these learner-leadership capabilities rarely develop at the same rate. A commitment to learner leadership requires seeking this balance and developing on both scales. Instead of becoming a *sophomore leader*, with more influence than understanding, continue developing into a *senior leader*. This will also require embracing *collaboration* as influence instead of *competition* as influence.

Appendix: Model Comparisons

This Appendix provides a list of 30 common change models which produce specific benefits when they align with the sensemaking pattern of story thinking. This comparison research found that there are two institutional models that do *not* align with the sensemaking pattern of story thinking: Policy-Making and Education (see Memorizing). In general, most models are prescriptive, in that they provide some memorized steps to perform. Now, with the comparisons made for each prescriptive model to the descriptive model of story thinking, specific alignments and gaps in sensemaking are provided.

These appendix models are compared under limited Fair Use copyright law for the purpose of commenting on their alignment with the pattern of story thinking, or the purpose of criticizing their misalignment with the pattern of story thinking.

List of Change Models

1. Agile Methodology
2. Bridges' Model
3. Change Management
4. Designing
5. Fixing
6. Holmes' Quote
7. Human Performance
8. Jugaad Innovation
9. Kotter's Model
10. Kubler-Ross' Model
11. Leading
12. Learning
13. Lewin's Model
14. Mapping Cycle
15. Memorizing
16. Policy-Making
17. Project Management
18. Research
19. Scientific Method
20. Scott/Jaffe's Model
21. Six Sigma DMAIC
22. Story Stages
23. Thinking
24. Trusting
25. Waterfall Methodology
26. ADDIE
27. CDIO
28. OODA
29. PDCA
30. SOAP

Agile Methodology

A non-linear approach to working based on fluid requirements (compare with Waterfall Methodology):

1. Requirements Analysis (Disruption and Investigation)
2. Design (Ideation)
3. Develop (Expectation)
4. Test (Affirmation)
5. Deploy (Expectation and Affirmation)
6. Maintain (Automation)

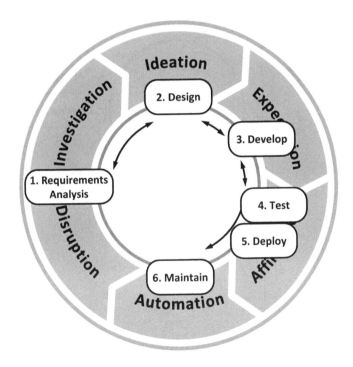

Bridges' Model

An approach to managing transitions of change:

1. Endings: From Does Work to Won't Work
2. Neutral Zone: From Won't Work to Could Work
3. Beginnings: From Could Work to Does Work

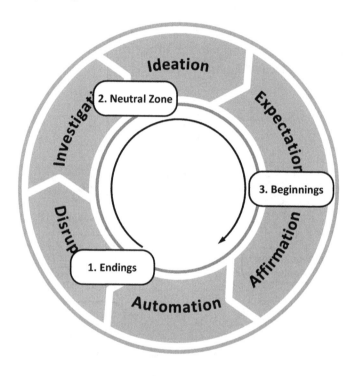

Change Management

The Change Management Process Groups, from the Association of Change Management Professionals (ACMP):

1. Evaluate Change Impact and Organizational Readiness (Disruption and Investigation)
2. Formulate the Change Management Strategy (Ideation)
3. Develop the Change Management Plan (Ideation)
4. Execute the Change Management Plan (Expectation)
5. Complete the Change Management Effort (Affirmation and Automation)

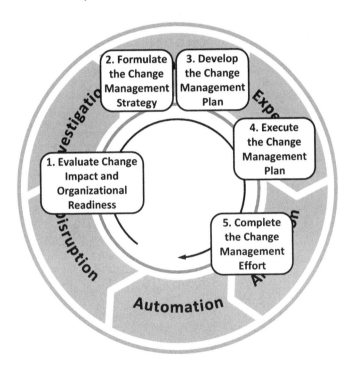

Designing

The steps for Design Thinking:

1. Empathize (Current State: Automation and Disruption)
2. Define (Disruption and Investigation)
3. Ideate (Ideation)
4. Prototype (Expectation)
5. Test (Affirmation)
6. Implement (Future State: Expectation, Affirmation and Automation)

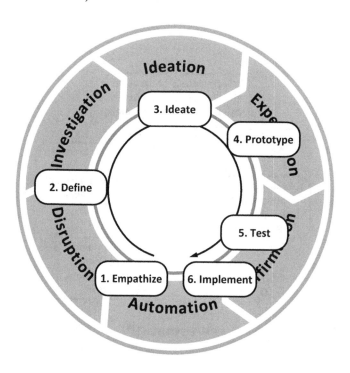

Fixing

The steps for Problem-Solving Thinking:
1. Symptom (Disruption)
2. Cause (Investigation)
3. Solution (Ideation)
4. Procedure (Expectation)
5. Check (Affirmation)

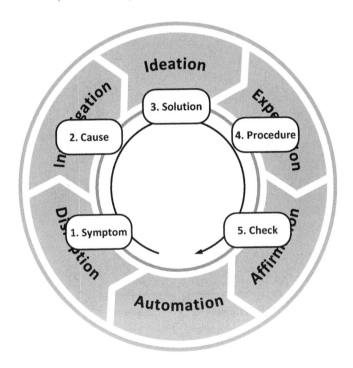

Holmes' Quote

Famous quote by Oliver Wendell Holmes: "I wouldn't give a fig for the simplicity on this side of complexity, but I would give my right arm for the simplicity on the far side of complexity."

1. Simplicity (Automation – Simplicity on this side of complexity)
2. Complexity (Disruption, Investigation, Ideation, Expectation, and Affirmation)
3. Elegance (Automation – Simplicity on the far side of complexity)

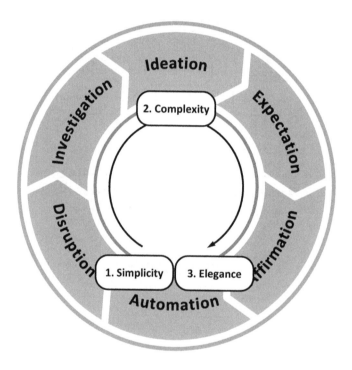

Human Performance

The Human Performance Improvement steps, from the International Society for Performance Improvement (ISPI):

1. Performance Analysis of Need or Opportunity (Disruption and Investigation)
2. Intervention Selection, Design, and Development (Ideation and Expectation)
3. Evaluation (Affirmation)
4. Intervention Implementation and Maintenance (Expectation, Affirmation, and Automation)

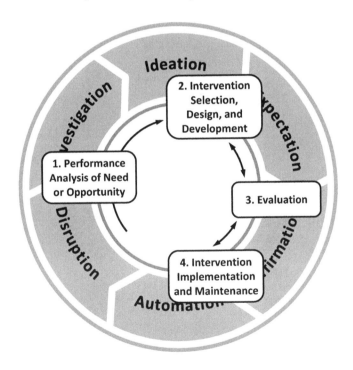

Jugaad Innovation

An approach to find more value using less resources (Frugal Innovation):

1. Be Bold: Find large issues, even those facing humanity (Disruption)
2. Seek the Available: Identify low-cost, high-access items (Investigation)
3. Repurpose: Idea's ingenuity based on reuse not creation (Ideation)

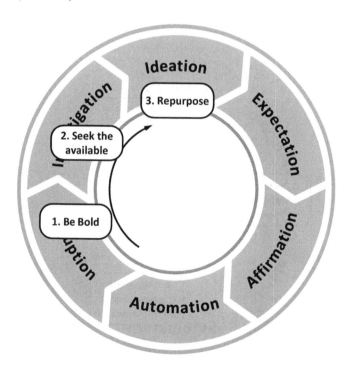

Kotter's Model

The eight steps of change:
1. Create / Increase Sense of Urgency (Disruption)
2. Form Coalition / Leadership Team (Disruption)
3. Create Strategic Vision (Ideation)
4. Gain Support of Workers (Expectation)
5. Remove Obstacles to Change (Expectation)
6. Create Short-Term Wins (Affirmation)
7. Leverage Wins / Credibility (Affirmation)
8. Institute Change in Culture (Automation)

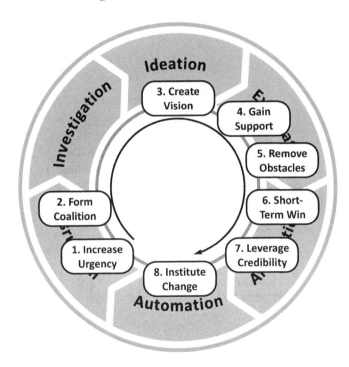

Kubler-Ross' Model

The Grief Change Sequence, published in, *On Death and Dying*:

1. Denial of the Disruption (Disruption)
2. Anger about the Disruption (Disruption)
3. Frustration of Feeling Stuck (Disruption and Investigation)
4. Depression of Won't Work (Investigation)
5. Exploration of Could Work (Investigation)
6. Decision to Move On (Ideation)
7. New Hope (Expectation)
8. New Confidence (Affirmation)
9. Integration into New Routine (Automation)

Leading

Transactional Leadership refers to Half-Pipe activities, where the primary goal is proficiency within Affirmation, Automation, and Disruption.

Transformational Leadership refers to Full-Cycle activities, where the primary goal is establishing a new routine and status quo. From the current routine and status quo (Automation), we lead others to see what won't work (Disruption) and the related questioning (Investigation), then lead others to derive what could work (Ideation) and build it (Expectation), and lead others to see what does work (Affirmation) and make it the new normal (Automation).

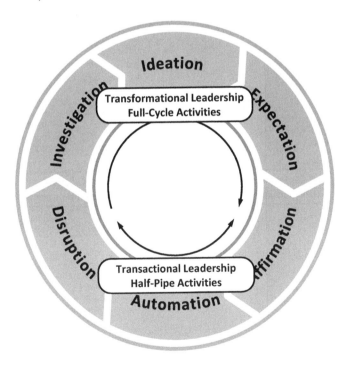

Learning

David A. Kolb is known for his observation of the learning process: Kolb's Experiential Learning Cycle (Cognitivism). His 4-stage cycle starts with immediate or concrete experiences, which provide a basis for reflective observations, which produce abstract concepts, which can be actively tested via experimentation.

1. Concrete Experience (Affirmation, Automation, and Disruption)
2. Reflective Observation (Investigation)
3. Abstract Conceptualization (Ideation)
4. Active Experimentation (Expectation and Affirmation)

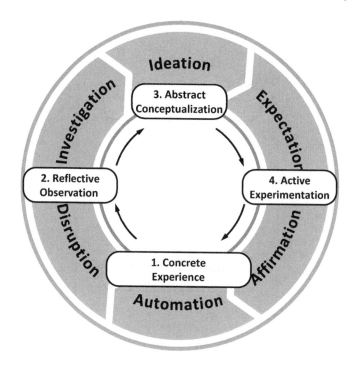

Lewin's Model

Lewin's change management model is an analogy based on changing the shape of a block of ice.

1. Unfreeze: From Reactive to Questioning
2. Change: From Could Work to Does Work
3. Refreeze: From Reflective to Reactive

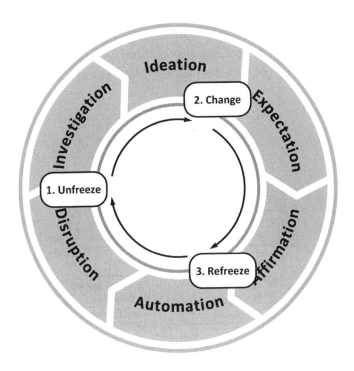

Mapping Cycle

The cycle of changing landscapes, map-making, and following directions. Note that the business and education landscapes have changed, yet we are still blindly following old directions:

1. Landscape has changed; People are lost (Disruption)
2. The landscape is surveyed (Investigation)
3. Map designs are considered (Ideation)
4. Maps are developed (Expectation)
5. Maps work; Directions are followed (Affirmation)
6. Directions are followed blindly (Automation)

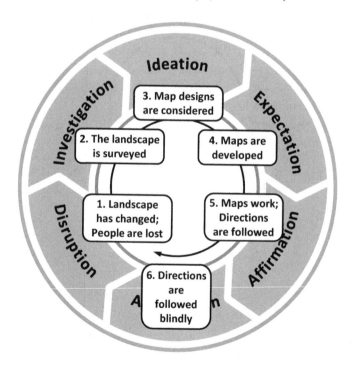

Memorizing

B.F. Skinner is known for his "Programmed Instruction" (Behaviorism) which produces Half-Pipe learning. His approach accelerates *instructional* outcomes by focusing on the desired *behavior*. Using "instructional objectives," the focus is on what works (for now), rather than preparing students with the skills needed when it won't work, and when it could work (Full-Cycle).

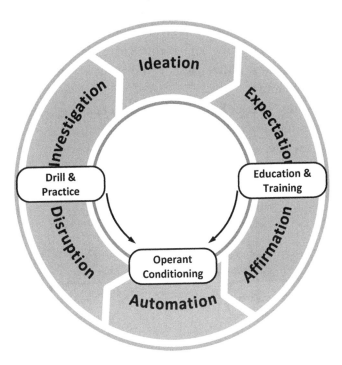

Policy-Making

This is the thinking process for creating a new policy (not politics):

1. Complaints: Interested party dissatisfied with status quo (Disruption)
2. Research: Determine root causes, or if expected known tradeoff (Investigation)
3. Ideas: Improvement ideas generated (Ideation)
4. Selection: Improvement idea selected (Ideation – submit bill**)
5. Support: Finding support (votes) for new idea (Expectation)
6. Agreement: Finding agreement (Affirmation – bill signed)
7. New Policy: Mandated routine (law) for status quo (Automation)

** Note: Listing "Submit Bill" as "Step 1" for creating a new law is not logical, yet is the usual way that we are taught about the process for creating a new law.

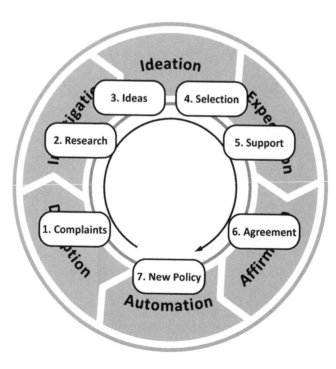

Project Management

The Five Process Groups for Project Management, from the Project Management Institute:

1. Initiating (Disruption and Investigation)
2. Planning (Investigation and Ideation)
3. Executing (Ideation and Expectation)
4. Monitoring and Controlling (Expectation and Affirmation)
5. Closing (Affirmation and Automation)

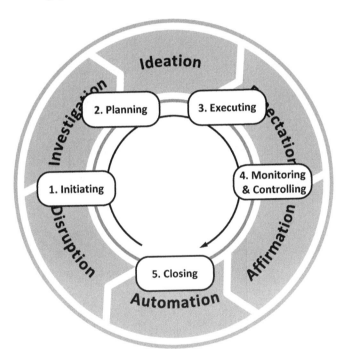

Research

Research is generally separated, in funding, expected timeframes, and company cultures, into Basic Research and Applied Research:

1. Basic Research (aka. Pure Research) (Disruption, Investigation, and Ideation)
2. Applied Research and Development (Ideation, Expectation, and Affirmation)
3. Operations (Affirmation, Automation, and Disruption)

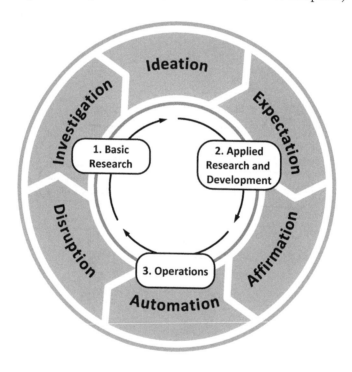

For an example, 1) Xerox invented the first PC with a Mouse and GUI in its labs (with 3 buttons); 2) Apple used the ideas to launch the Lisa and then the Macintosh personal computers (with 1 button); and 3) Microsoft made the mouse and graphical user interface the industry norm (2 buttons). See the book, *Fumbling the Future: How Xerox Invented, Then Ignored, The First Personal Computer* (Smith and Alexander, 1999).

Scientific Method

The scientific method of research:
1. Make Observations (Disruption)
2. Ask Questions (Investigation)
3. Formulate Hypothesis (Ideation)
4. Test Predictions for Empirical Replicability (Expectation)
5. Draw Conclusions (Affirmation)
6. Communicate Results (Affirmation and Automation)

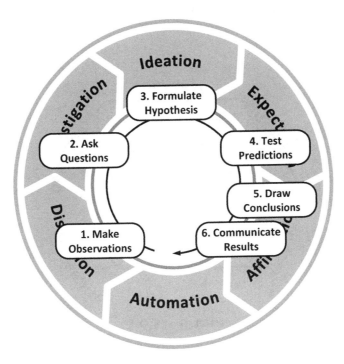

Scott/Jaffe's Model

The stages of change, from the Scott/Jaffe model:

1. Deny: Reject reality of Disruption (Disruption)
2. Resist: Oppose management strategies for Disruption (Disruption)
3. Explore: Questioning for Investigation and Ideation (Investigation and Ideation)
4. Commit: Begin to take action in Expectation (Expectation, Affirmation, and Automation)

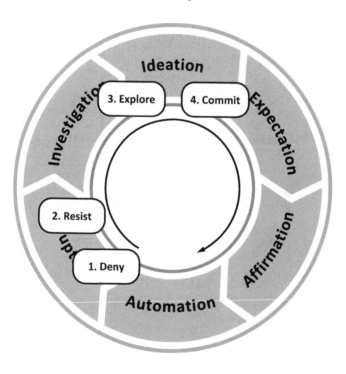

Six Sigma DMAIC

An approach to reduce defects in manufacturing processes, using the DMAIC thinking model:

1. Define: Define disruption as a problem (not opportunity) (Disruption)
2. Measure: Measure production variation from expected (Disruption)
3. Analyze: Use statistical methods to find root causes (Investigation)
4. Improve: Create new ideas and implement plan (Ideation, Expectation, and Affirmation)
5. Control: Reduce production variations to less than 3 defects per million units (6 sigma measurement) (Automation)

Note: "LEAN" is a Half-Pipe operations strategy, commonly combined with Six Sigma (in Control), to add production value with fewer resources.

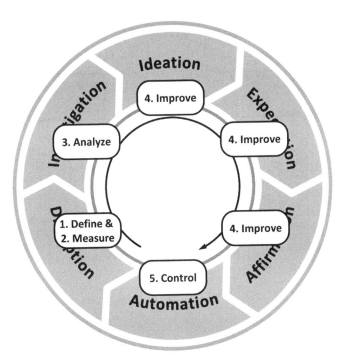

Story Stages

The structure of the generic story includes these stages:

1. Exposition: The background and current routine (Automation)
2. Desperation: The conflict, chaos, or boredom (Disruption)
3. Revelation: The search for answers (Investigation)
4. Consideration: The objective defined (meet with mentor) (Ideation)
5. Determination: The effort of working the plan (Expectation)
6. Resolution: The reward, restoration, or confirmation (Affirmation)
7. Transformation: The new identity and routine (Automation)

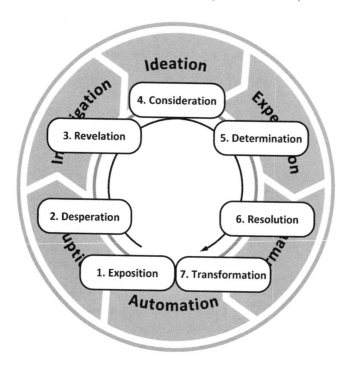

Thinking

Based on Daniel Kahneman's book, *Thinking Fast and Slow*, individuals and organizations have two modes of thinking, called "Fast and Slow." Thinking *Fast* refers to Half-Pipe activities, where we cite answers in Affirmation and react to Disruptions, while primarily staying in Automation (routine).

Thinking *Slow* refers to Full-Cycle activities, where we move through all 6 phases of change and *evaluate* new solutions/answers in Affirmation (confirm), rather than just *citing* answers (affirm). This distinction between fast and slow is captured within organization charts that begin with just two boxes: "Operations" and "R&D."

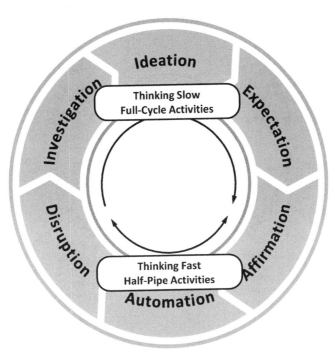

Trusting

The phrase, "Trust but Verify" describes a strategy used between countries, where agreements are trusted, but also later verified.

We can reach Affirmation quickly in the Half-Pipe by simply ceding to some authority, citing an answer, and trusting the source and answer. But with the Full-Cycle, we reach Affirmation only after we prioritize the problem within Disruption, question ways and means within Investigation and Ideation, and develop and execute methods of evaluation within Expectation and Affirmation.

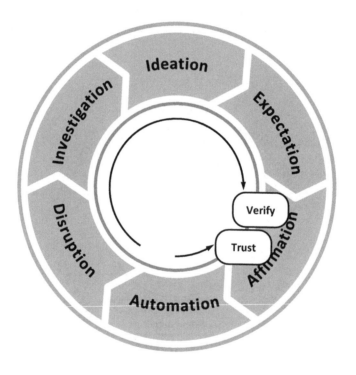

Waterfall Methodology

A linear approach to working based on fixed requirements (compare with Agile Methodology):

1. Requirements Determined (Disruption and Investigation)
2. Design (Ideation)
3. Develop (Expectation)
4. Test (Affirmation)
5. Deploy (Expectation and Affirmation)
6. Maintain (Automation)

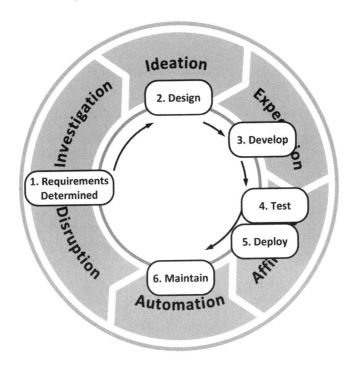

The waterfall philosophy is that once one step is complete, we move down to the next step, as in a waterfall. But in organizations with learning environments, we learn new things that require that we return momentarily to the previous step, like salmon swimming back upstream. This requires the arrows going in both directions and is called an Agile Methodology.

ADDIE

ADDIE is an Instructional Design Process for Educators and Trainers:

1. Analysis: Determine human performance gaps (Investigation)
2. Design: Determine performance intervention (Ideation)
3. Development: Develop intervention (Expectation)
4. Implementation: Implement intervention (Expectation and Affirmation)
5. Evaluation: Evaluate intervention (Affirmation)

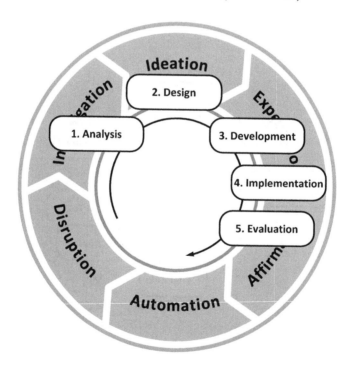

CDIO

CDIO is an Educational Framework for Engineers:
1. Conceive (Disruption and Investigation)
2. Design (Ideation)
3. Implement (Expectation and Affirmation)
4. Operate (Automation, Disruption, and Affirmation)

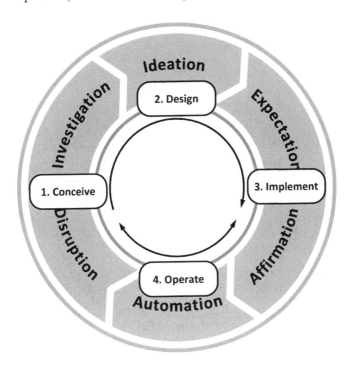

OODA

OODA is a Decision Cycle:

1. Observe (Affirmation, Automation, and Disruption)
2. Orient (Investigation)
3. Decide (Ideation)
4. Act (Expectation)

Note: This decision cycle can also occur *within* each phase of change.

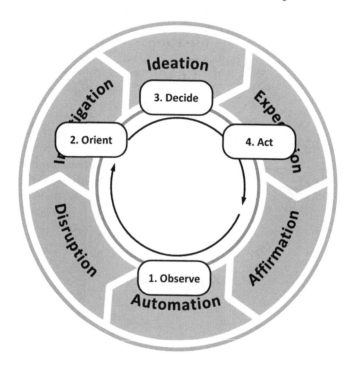

PDCA

Plan-Do-Check-Act is an iterative four-step management method for continuous improvement:

1. Plan: Establish objectives and create a plan of action (Ideation)
2. Do: Implement the plan (Expectation)
3. Check: Compare actual results with expected results (Affirmation)
4. Act: Investigate reasons why results are not as expected (Investigation)

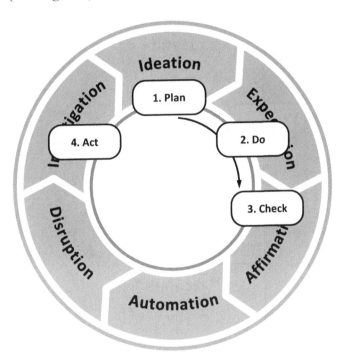

SOAP

SOAP is a thinking and documentation model used in healthcare:

1. Subjective: The patient's complaint of problem/symptom (Disruption)
2. Objective: The healthcare provider's initial observation (Disruption)
3. Assessment: A medical diagnosis/analysis (Investigation)
4. Plan: The strategy for treatment (Ideation)

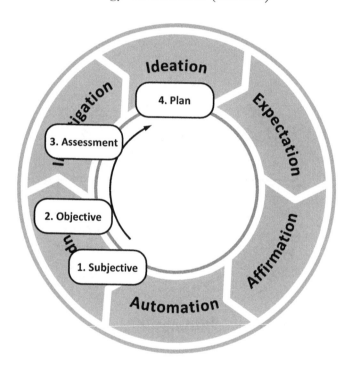

Acknowledgments

The origins of this book, in the study of mental models, first began nearly two decades ago within my doctoral dissertation in educational psychology. For this, I thank the faculty in the School of Education at the University of Southern California. For their diligence in reviewing my manuscript and providing valuable insights, I am extremely grateful to Bill Adams, Natasha Adams, Dr. Anthony J. DiBella, Stan Garfield, Timothy S. Griles, Dr. Art Murray, Eric F. Palmer, and Ralph Poole. I am especially grateful to my wife, Mary, and my children, Shannon, and Jonathan, for their support, encouragement, and always-constructive feedback on my ideas, including those that did not make their way into this book, and for their review of the early manuscript drafts.

Selected Bibliography

Anderson, E. 1987. *Preoperative preparation for cardiac surgery facilitates recovery, reduces psychological distress, and reduces the incidence of acute postoperative hypertension.* Journal of Consulting and Clinical Psychology – Vol. 55 No. 4, 513-520.

Anderson, L., Krathwohl, D., et al. 2001. *A taxonomy for learning, teaching, and assessing: A revision of Bloom's taxonomy of educational objectives.* Brooklyn: Pearson.

Argyris, C. Sept 1977. *Double loop learning in organizations,* Harvard Business Review, (pp. 115–124).

Ariely, A. 2008. *Predictably irrational: The hidden forces that shape our decisions.* New York: HarperCollins.

Arndt, M., and B. Einhorn. April 15, 2010. *The 50 most innovative companies.* Businessweek.

Ashby, W.R. 1964. *An introduction to cybernetics* (2nd ed.) London: Methuen & Co Ltd.

Barker, J. A. 1993. *Paradigms: The business of discovering the future.* New York: Harper Business.

Bass, B. M. 1990. *From transactional to transformational leadership: Learning to share the vision,* Organizational Dynamics, (Winter): 19-31.

Bennet, A., and D. Bennet. 2004. *Organizational survival in the new world: The intelligent complex adaptive system.* Boston: KMCI Press.

Bennet, A., Bennet, D., & Lewis, J. Aug 2015. *Leading with the future in mind: Knowledge and emergent leadership.* The New Reality Series. Frost, WV: MQI Press.

Bennet, A., Bennet, D., Shelley, A., Bullard, T., & Lewis, J. Jan 2017. *The profundity and bifurcation of change*. Frost, WV: MQI Press.

Bernerth, J., Walker, H., Harris, S. Dec 2011. *Change fatigue: Development and initial validation of a new measure*, Work & Stress - International Journal of Work, Health & Organisations, 25(4): 321-337.

Bloom, A. 1987. *The closing of the American mind: How higher education has failed democracy and impoverished the souls of today's students*. New York: Simon & Schuster.

Bloom, B. 1956. *Taxonomy of educational objectives, Handbook 1: Cognitive Domain*. White Plains: Longman.

Blumenfeld, S., and Newman, A. 2015. *Crimes of the educators*. Washington, D.C.: WND Books.

Cacioppo, J.T.; Petty, R.E.; Kao, C.F. 1984. *The efficient assessment of need for cognition*. Journal of Personality Assessment. 48 (3): 306–307.

Cambridge University Press. (2019). *Cambridge online dictionary*, Cambridge Dictionary online.

Chomsky, N. 1997. *Media control: The spectacular achievements of propaganda*. Seven Stories Press.

Collins, J. 2001. *Good to great: Why some companies make the leap and others don't*. New York: HarperCollins Publishers.

Cooperrider, D., and Whitney, D. 2005. *Appreciative inquiry: A positive revolution in change*. San Francisco: Berrett-Koehler Publishers, Inc.

Davenport, T. Jan 2008. *Why six sigma is on the downslope*, Harvard Business Review Blog Network.

de Geus, A. 1997. *The living company: Habits for survival in a turbulent business environment*. Boston: Longview Publishing.

Dixon, N. 1999. *The organizational learning cycle: How we can learn collectively*. U.K.: McGraw Hill.

Dunning, D. 2011. *Advances in experimental social psychology: Chapter five – The Dunning-Kruger effect: On being ignorant of one's own ignorance*. New York: Elsevier.

Fletcher, P. C., Happe´, F., Frith, U., et al. 1995. *Other minds in the brain: a functional imaging study of "theory of mind" in story comprehension*. Cognition 57:109 –128.

Fritz, R. 1989. *Path of least resistance: Learning to become the creative force in your life.* New York: Fawcett Books.

Gano, D. L. 2008. *Apollo root cause analysis.* Richland: Apollonian Publications.

Gentner, D., and Stevens, A. L. 1983. *Mental models.* Hillsdale: Lawrence Erlbaum Associates.

Goldratt, E. M. 1984. *The goal: A process of ongoing improvement.* Great Barrington: North River Press.

Goleman, D. 1995. *Emotional intelligence: Why it can matter more than IQ.* New York: Bantam Books.

Griffin, J., and I. Tyrrell. 2003. *Human givens: A new approach to emotional health and clear thinking.* East Sussex: HG Publishing.

Haidt, J. 2006. *The happiness hypothesis: Finding modern truth in ancient wisdom.* New York: Basic Books.

Hammond, K. R. 1996. *Human judgment and social policy: Irreducible uncertainty, inevitable error, unavoidable injustice.* New York: Oxford University Press.

Iserbyt, C. 1999. *The deliberate dumbing down of America.* Ravenna: Conscience Press.

Jacoby, S. 2008. *The age of American unreason.* New York: Random House.

Jonassen, D. H., K. Beissner, and M. Yacci. 1993. *Structural knowledge: Techniques for representing, conveying, and acquiring structural knowledge.* Hillsdale: Lawrence Erlbaum Associates.

Kahneman, D. 2011. *Thinking fast and slow.* New York: Farrar, Straus and Giroux.

Kellogg, R. T. 1995. *Cognitive psychology.* Thousand Oaks: Sage Publications.

Kelly, K. January 2013. *Robots are coming to take our jobs.* Wired.

Kern, F. May 18, 2010. *What chief executives really want.* Businessweek.

Kieras, D. E. 1988. *What mental model should be taught: Choosing instructional content for complex engineered systems.* In J. Psotka, L. D. Massey, & S. A. Mutter (Eds.), Intelligent tutoring systems, 85-111. Hillsdale, NJ: Lawrence Erlbaum Associates.

Klein, G., Ross, K, Moon, B. et al. May/June 2003. *Macrocognition, Intelligent Systems.*

Kolb, D. A. 1976. *On management and the learning process*, California Management Review, 18(3): 21-31.

Kotter, John P. 1998. *Leading change: Why transformation efforts fail.* In Harvard Business Review on Change. Pp. 1-20. Boston: Harvard Business School Press. (Originally published in HBR 1995 (March-April)).

Krathwohl, D. R. Autumn 2002. *A revision of Bloom's taxonomy: An overview*, Theory Into Practice, 41(4):212-218.

Krauthammer, C. 2013. *Things that matter: Three decades of passions, pastimes and politics.* New York: Penguin Random House.

Kubler-Ross, E. 1969. *On death and dying.* New York: Macmillan Publishing Company.

Kuhlmann, H. 2005. *Living Walden Two: B. F. Skinner's behaviorist utopia and experimental communities.* University of Illinois.

Kuhn, T. 1962. *The structure of scientific revolutions.* Chicago: University of Chicago Press.

Lazarus, R. & Smith, C. 1988. *Knowledge and appraisal in the cognition—emotion relationship.* Cognition and Emotion, 2:4, 281-300.

Lewis, J. 2013. *The explanation age – 3rd ed.*, Amazon.

Lewis, J. Oct 2013. *The ADIIEA Cycle: Creating an integrated framework for business processes and organizational learning*, Paper presented at The International Conference on Intellectual Capital, Knowledge Management and Organizational Learning (ICICKM), The George Washington University, Washington D.C. (pp. 228-235).

Lewis, J. June 2014. *ADIIEA: An organizational learning model for business management and innovation*, The Electronic Journal of Knowledge Management – Volume 12 Issue 2 (pp 98-107).

Malmkjaer, K. 1996. *The linguistics encyclopedia.* New York: Routledge.

Marr, B. July 15 2019. *The future of work: 5 important ways jobs will change in the 4th industrial revolution.* Forbes.

Martin, R. December 21, 2009. *Uranium is so last century—Enter thorium, the new green nuke.* Wired.

Maslow, A. H. 1943. *A theory of human motivation.* Psychological Review, 50(4), 370-396.

Maybee, J. E. Winter 2016. *Hegel's dialectics,* The Stanford Encyclopedia of Philosophy, Edward N. Zalta (ed.), URL = <https://plato.stanford.edu/archives/win2016/entries/hegel-dialectics/>

Mayer, R. E. 1989. Models for understanding. Review of Educational Research, 59(1), 43-64.

McGinn, D. November 16, 2009. *The decline of Western innovation.* Newsweek.

McGinnis, J. R., and D. Roberts-Harris. September/October 2009. *A new vision for teaching science.* Scientific American Mind.

Mercier, H., and Sperber, D. 2017. *The enigma of reason.* Cambridge: Harvard University Press.

Merrill, M. D. 1983. *Component display theory.* In C. Reigeluth (ed.), Instructional design theories and models. Hillsdale: Erlbaum Associates.

Nonaka, I., and H. Takeuchi. 1995. *The knowledge-creating company: How Japanese companies create the dynamics of innovation.* New York: Oxford University Press.

Ochsner, K., Bunge, S., Gross, J., Gabrieli, J. 2002. *Rethinking feelings: An fMRI study of the cognitive regulation of emotion.* Journal of Cognitive Neuroscience 14:8, pp. 1215–1229.

Paul, Richard W. 1995. *Critical thinking: How to prepare students for a rapidly changing world.* Jane Willsen and A.J.A. Binker, eds., Santa Rosa, CA: Foundation for Critical Thinking.

Peale, N. V. 2003. *The power of positive thinking.* New York: Prentice-Hall.

Pink, D. H. 2005. *A whole new mind: Moving from the information age to the conceptual age.* New York: Riverhead Books.

Richelle, M. N. 1993. *B. F. Skinner: A reappraisal.* East Sussex: Lawrence Erlbaum Associates Ltd.

Rouse, W. B., & Morris, N. M. 1986. *On looking into the black box: Prospects and limits in the search for mental models.* Psychological Bulletin 100 (3), 349-363.

Schwab, K. 2017. *The fourth industrial revolution.* New York: Crown Publishing.

Seligman, M. E. P. 2002. *Authentic happiness.* New York: Free Press.

Senge, P. Fall 1990. *The leader's new work: Building learning organizations,* MIT Sloan School of Management.

Senge, P. 2006. *The fifth discipline: The art and practice of the learning organization.* New York: Doubleday.

Shankar, R. 2009. *Process improvement using six sigma: A DMAIC guide.* Milwaukee: American Society for Quality, Quality Press.

Sinek, S. 2009. *Start with why.* London: Penguin Books Ltd.

Sinek, S., Mead, D., and Docker, P. 2017. *Find your why.* New York: Penguin Random House.

Skinner, B. F. 1953. *Science and human behavior.* New York: The Free Press.

Skinner, B. F. 1971. *Beyond freedom and dignity.* Indianapolis: Hackett Publishing.

Smith, D., Alexander, R. 1999. *Fumbling the future: How Xerox invented, then ignored, the first personal computer.* Lincoln, NE: toExcel Publishing.

Stolovitch, H. D. and E. J. Keeps, eds. 1992. *Handbook of human performance technology.* San Francisco: Jossey-Bass.

Teasdale, K. 1993. *Information and anxiety: A critical reappraisal.* Journal of Advanced Nursing – 18, 1125-1132.

Thagard, P. 2005. *Mind: Introduction to cognitive science.* Cambridge: MIT Press.

Thomas, K. W. 2002. *Intrinsic motivation at work: Building energy and commitment.* San Francisco: Berrett-Koehler.

Tosey, P., Visser, M., & Saunders, M. Dec 2011. *The origins and conceptualizations of 'triple-loop' learning: A critical review.* Management Learning.

Tufte, E. R. 1997. *Visual explanations: Images and quantities, evidence and narrative.* Cheshire: Graphics Press.

Twardy, C. R. 2003. *Argument maps improve critical thinking.* Teaching Philosophy.

United States National Commission on Excellence in Education 1983. *A nation at risk: The imperative for educational reform.*

Weick, K. 1995. *Sensemaking in organizations.* Thousand Oaks: Sage Publications.

Williams, M. 2001. *Problems of knowledge: A critical introduction to epistemology.* Oxford: Oxford University Press.

Wilson, E. O. 1998. *Consilience: The unity of knowledge.* New York: Alfred A. Knopf, Inc.

Wurman, R. S. 1989. *Information anxiety.* New York: Doubleday.

Xenophon and H. Morley, eds. 2007. *The memorable thoughts of Socrates.* Charleston: BiblioBazaar.